"Clark calls missionaries and the churches that support them to faithful ministry that looks to God's approval and to the reward God gives. We are so quick to live for the praise of people instead of the praise of God. Clark also corrects the idea that Paul invariably planted churches and then moved quickly on to the next field. Instead, we see that Paul continued to labor and work with churches so that they were established in truth. I would love to see every missionary and every church sending and supporting missionaries (which should be all churches!) read this book."

Thomas R. Schreiner, James Buchanan Harrison Professor of New Testament Interpretation, The Southern Baptist Theological Seminary

"*Mission Affirmed* is immensely practical, challenging, accessible, and hopeful. It is a call to be more thoroughly and thoughtfully biblical about why we do the things we do in missions. All of us—whether pastors or church members, goers or senders—could all benefit from this insightful book."

Gloria Furman, author, *Missional Motherhood*; coeditor, *Joyfully Spreading the Word*

"The greatest dangers facing the church are internal, but they're not always obvious. In *Mission Affirmed*, Elliot Clark reminds us of an unnoticed, even celebrated, danger undermining our mission—the lure of selfish motivations and worldly means to accomplish the Great Commission. Instead, Clark argues, we must embrace Paul's eschatological motivation. Paul's longing to be approved by God on the last day fueled his missionary desire and guided his missiological methods. By recovering Paul's motivation for missions, we, too, will long to please the God who has already accepted us in Christ by his grace, and we will eschew the praise of others. Churches, pastors, Christians, missionaries, sending agencies—we all need this vital reminder."

Juan Sanchez, Senior Pastor, High Pointe Baptist Church, Austin, Texas; author, *The Leadership Formula*

T0327302

"Elliot Clark is unafraid to poke at sleeping bears in the world of missions. Are current mission movements biblical? Should we translate the Bible so that it is more palatable to those of other faiths? Are sending churches scrupulous about those they send? For answers, Clark looks to missiologists, missionaries old and new, and his own personal examples, but most of all, thankfully, Clark zeroes in on the apostle Paul and his work in the early church. From Paul's examples, Clark issues both warnings and helpful corrections so that we will not be disqualified as we run the race of missions."

J. Mack Stiles, missionary and former pastor in the Middle East; author, *Evangelism*

Mission Affirmed

Other Gospel Coalition Books

Mission Affirmed

Recovering the Missionary Motivation of Paul

Elliot Clark

CROSSWAY®

WHEATON, ILLINOIS

Mission Affirmed: Recovering the Missionary Motivation of Paul
Copyright © 2022 by Elliot Clark
Published by Crossway
   1300 Crescent Street
   Wheaton, Illinois 60187
All rights reserved. No part of this publication may be reproduced, stored in a retrieval system, or transmitted in any form by any means, electronic, mechanical, photocopy, recording, or otherwise, without the prior permission of the publisher, except as provided for by USA copyright law. Crossway® is a registered trademark in the United States of America.
Cover design: Jordan Singer
Cover image: Bridgeman Images
First printing 2022
Printed in the United States of America
Scripture quotations are from the ESV® Bible (The Holy Bible, English Standard Version®), copyright © 2001 by Crossway, a publishing ministry of Good News Publishers. Used by permission. All rights reserved.
All emphases in Scripture quotations have been added by the author.
Trade paperback ISBN: 978-1-4335-7380-4
ePub ISBN: 978-1-4335-7383-5
PDF ISBN: 978-1-4335-7381-1
Mobipocket ISBN: 978-1-4335-7382-8

Library of Congress Cataloging-in-Publication Data
Names: Clark, Elliot, author.
Title: Mission affirmed : recovering the missionary motivation of Paul / Elliot Clark.
Description: Wheaton, Illinois : Crossway, [2022] | Includes bibliographical references and index.
Identifiers: LCCN 2021015192 (print) | LCCN 2021015193 (ebook) | ISBN 9781433573804 (trade paperback) | ISBN 9781433573811 (pdf) | ISBN 9781433573828 (mobi) | ISBN 9781433573835 (epub)
Subjects: LCSH: Bible. Epistles of Paul—Theology. | Mission of the church.| Missions—Biblical teaching. | Paul, the Apostle, Saint.
Classification: LCC BS2655.M57 C53 2022 (print) | LCC BS2655.M57 (ebook) | DDC 230—dc23
LC record available at https://lccn.loc.gov/2021015192
LC ebook record available at https://lccn.loc.gov/2021015193

Crossway is a publishing ministry of Good News Publishers.

VP		32	31	30	29	28	27	26	25	24	23	22
15	14	13	12	11	10	9	8	7	6	5	4	3	2	1

To the honor of my missionary heroes,
whose good and faithful service
produces thanksgiving in me
to the glory of God

SPAIN →

Rome

MACEDONIA   Phili
        Berea
            Thessaloni

    GREECE   Aeg
                     S

        Corinth ◆ Athens
ACHAIA Cenchreae

                    CRET

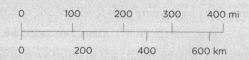

0   100   200   300   400 mi

0   200   400   600 km

roas

ASIA

GALATIA

Ephesus
◆

PISIDIA

Miletus
◆

LYCAONIA

Tarsus
◆

CILICIA

◆ Antioch

CYPRUS

SYRIA

Mediterranean Sea

◆ Damascus

NABATEA

JUDEA ◆ Jerusalem

ARABIA

Contents

Introduction

More Than Mission Accomplished

Troas

FROM THE DISTANT HORIZON, ships trace into the turquoise harbor like bees on blue sky returning to their hive. They come to Troas from across the Mediterranean Basin and funnel northward, following the Aegean to this, the westernmost tip of Asia. From here, not far across the watery divide, stands Greece and the heart of the Roman Empire. Troas is a place where East meets the sea, and where the sea opens westward to opportunity. This port city is the perfect launchpad for European expedition.

So it was for Paul, for it was here where the apostle, during his second missionary journey, first received a vision summoning him to Macedonia (Acts 16:6–10), a call for help that propelled the gospel into Europe, all the way to the glorious cities of Athens and Corinth. That seminal moment, "the Macedonian Call," has since become metaphorical for the task of Christian missions and archetypal of Paul's ambition as a pioneer evangelist.

Perhaps that missionary compulsion led Paul back to Troas on his third journey. After spending nearly three years in Asia Minor's

Ephesus working at his trade, teaching daily in the hall of Tyrannus, and ministering in private homes, Paul was ready to move on. He desired to return and visit the believers in Macedonia and Greece, retracing his steps—as was his custom. His excursion would again begin in Troas.

In a letter to the Corinthian church, Paul tells the story of that second visit to Troas. "A door was opened for me in the Lord" (2 Cor. 2:12)—Paul's way of saying that the power of God's Spirit was on display as people heard and believed the gospel (Acts 14:27). Here again, this metaphor is one Christians still employ today. Missionaries, following Paul's example, long and pray for such an occasion, for a door to be opened to declare the message of Christ (Col. 4:3).

Striking, though, is what Paul recounts next. That moment—when the Holy Spirit was at work and the gospel was bearing fruit—Paul left.

As my teenaged son would say, "Wait, what?" What could lead Paul, the pioneer missionary with a driving passion to reach the unreached, to walk away from an open door? What was it that, while not incredibly urgent, became for Paul more important?

From his letter to the Corinthians, we discover that Paul had apparently come to Troas with multiple intentions. Among them, he wanted to preach the gospel. But Troas was a rendezvous point. Paul was there waiting for his colleague, Titus, likely due any day onboard a ship from Corinth.[1] And Paul was concerned about the news he would bring. Had the Corinthian church received Paul's message and his messenger? How did they

---

1 For a summary of the events preceding the composition of 2 Corinthians, see David E. Garland, *2 Corinthians* (Nashville: B&H, 1999), 26–30.

respond to the apostle's stinging rebuke? Was their relationship intact or in ruins?

Perhaps every so often Paul would venture out onto the docks or ascend the craggy cliffs overlooking Troas's harbor and spy for the latest ship arriving from the West. As time wore on and Titus didn't show, Paul says he became unsettled. Despite the incredible opportunity for witness before him, anxiety grew within him (2 Cor. 2:12–13). He was disturbed to the point of abandoning Troas—again, for a second time.

Evangelization of the World in Our Lifetime

As early as 1900, at the turn of the last century, John R. Mott put to page what had already become the rallying cry of the Student Volunteer Movement for Foreign Missions: "The Evangelization of the World in This Generation."[2] As a burgeoning Protestant organization made up of ambitious young people from Western nations such as the United States, Canada, Great Britain, and Ireland, these students saw the urgent global need and unprecedented opportunity to take the gospel to the whole world in their lifetimes. They believed it could be done.

Looking back on these youthful forebears from an optimistic era, we might be tempted to snicker at such audacity. With the clarity of hindsight, we can now see how that vision was destined for failure. In fact, we could note that the glowing enthusiasm of many Protestants in that day didn't materialize into global evangelization but, instead, faded in the shadows of world wars.

Yet from the darkness of World War II a new generation of missionaries and strategists emerged that once again roused the church

---

2   John R. Mott, *The Evangelization of the World in This Generation* (New York: Student Volunteer Movement for Foreign Missions, 1900).

to consider her role in the world and the possibility of reaching the uttermost parts of the earth. Perhaps the foremost proponent of this vision was Ralph Winter, professor at the School of World Mission at Fuller Seminary, who, along with Donald McGavran, inspired a new generation of Christian ambassadors and simultaneously raised the stakes for the church's mission. At Lausanne I in 1974, the First International Congress on World Evangelization, Winter brought the world's "hidden peoples" into view, broadening the Great Commission call to reach all nations—previously understood as geopolitical nation states—by unveiling the lostness of ethnolinguistic people groups. The insight and writing of McGavran and Winter infused missions with a fresh urgency while inspiring a renewed optimism. Once those people groups had been located, the task would become definable and therefore attainable.[3]

Today, we're still riding the wave of that transformative vision. In subsequent decades, countless ministries and organizations have made it their ambition to identify, classify, and reach the unreached. With scientific precision we've now determined the scope of our mission, and we're increasingly motivated by the possibility of its accomplishment. The missions community is once again buoyed by the hope of "finishing the task." Like John Mott and the Student Volunteer Movement of that bygone era, many today are convinced that we'll see the completion of the missionary mandate within our lifetimes. It's all within reach.[4]

3 For example: "In the 1970s, the Lord began to open the eyes of many to the fact that the irreducible, essential mission task of a breakthrough in every people group was also a completable task." See Ralph D. Winter and Bruce A. Koch, "Finishing the Task: The Unreached Peoples Challenge," Joshua Project website, accessed April 10, 2020, joshuaproject.net/assets/media/articles/finishing-the-task.pdf, 539.

4 Others have questioned this perspective, and a growing number of missiologists and mission agencies are rethinking the way we designate people groups. See Peter T. Lee and James

But what does this have to do with Paul leaving Troas?

Many Christians assume a narrative of the apostle's ministry: that his singular ambition was to preach the gospel to those who hadn't heard, in lands yet unreached.[5] In extreme cases, Paul can be presented as not much more than a one-dimensional character from a mass market paperback. According to this reading, all he cared about was the next city, the next people group, the final frontier. To be fair, the book of Acts can contribute somewhat to this assumption, as Luke's story races along with Paul scurrying from one location to the next. And when we read Paul's letter to the church in Rome—a city he had yet to visit—we find him already talking about the next destination, Spain.

But Troas—and Paul's tenuous and tear-filled relationship with the church at Corinth—presents another dimension. Paul's ministry was motivated by more than the pioneer advance of the gospel.[6] The anxiety he felt about Corinth was common to his experience with multiple churches (2 Cor. 11:28). He was constantly concerned with issues of ecclesial unity, moral purity, theological accuracy, and leadership development. Paul's goal wasn't just to preach the gospel but to teach the whole counsel of God and present everyone mature in Christ (Acts 20:27; Col. 1:28). Paul was a goer and, sometimes when possible, a stayer. He also devoted significant time to his tentmaking vocation and, when necessary, defended his

Sung-Hwan Park, "Beyond People Group Thinking: A Critical Reevaluation of Unreached People Groups," *Missiology: An International Review* 46, no. 3 (2018): 212–25.

5 Paul's stated ambition "to preach the gospel, not where Christ has already been named" (Rom. 15:20) doesn't preclude the reality that he had multiple aims in his apostolic ministry.

6 Dean Gilliland acknowledges that "the work for spiritual conversion had prior claim on Paul's life," yet there are many aspects of his holistic ministry that the Bible describes in ways "so matter-of-fact that it would be easy to miss" the various features of Paul's mission. See Dean S. Gilliland, *Pauline Theology and Mission Practice* (Grand Rapids, MI: Baker, 1983), 65.

personal reputation (Acts 18:1–3; cf. 20:33–35). In the last years of his ministry, he even invested much effort and relational capital to provide for the poor believers in Jerusalem (1 Cor. 16:1–4; 2 Cor. 8:1–9:15; Rom. 15:25–32), not just to raise support for his mission to the remote boundaries of the Mediterranean.

Perhaps most overlooked of all, Paul was motivated by the approval of God. As he mentions repeatedly in his Corinthian correspondence, his driving ambition—one of many—was to receive, on the last day, God's commendation (1 Cor. 4:5; 2 Cor. 5:9–10; 10:18). This pursuit of God's praise, while of critical importance, also led Paul to seek the affirmation of others, including his church plants. If they moved on from the apostle and his teaching, Paul was concerned for their position before Christ. If other teachers emerged who didn't build appropriately on the foundation Paul laid, he knew it spelled disaster. And it was this concern—an issue Titus was bringing word about—that pulled Paul away from a wide-open door for evangelism. So, whatever we might assume about Paul's priorities in mission and his zealous ambition for reaching the unreached, we must also take his anxious departure from Troas into account. In a sense, it was a kind of reverse Macedonian call.

Missions in an Age of Two-Day Delivery and Disposable Culture

I'll never forget the phone call that changed my view of missions forever. Our family was living in one of the most unreached pockets of one of the most unreached nations in the world. When we'd first moved to the Central Asian city that we called home, the nearest church was five hours away. You could jump in a car and drive for hundreds of miles in any direction, passing innumerable towns and villages, knowing that every single person you saw was

Muslim. Not only were the people not Christian, but they'd likely never heard a clear explanation of the gospel—and they had little prospect of hearing it anytime soon.

As I would travel throughout this region, I was always struck by the vastness of its lostness, a reality tauntingly echoed by the rambling, windswept mountains across the endless, treeless steppe. The land was barren, sun-scorched, and thirsty for the gospel. The indescribable need led us to plant our family there.

But here I was, on the phone with my colleague and supervisor, letting him know we'd decided to move on. I could list all the reasons I gave him, but they're not essential to this telling. What's important to know is that we felt compelled by circumstance and by God's Spirit to leave.

In our relatively short time in that city, God had blessed. Some had come to faith. Some were baptized. We had a small congregation gathering regularly for worship—a church in embryonic form. While our leaving wouldn't necessarily terminate the life of that body, I knew it would severely threaten its viability. A few of the believers had already moved elsewhere for university or to follow work opportunities. Among those who stayed, we were facing internal strife and division, due in part to fears of police infiltration—from within our small group. This had shaken the confidence of all, but especially the newest believers whose faith was fragile. We also sensed that the government would soon deny residency to the few other missionaries on our team. Our labor of love was in real jeopardy.

As I communicated this situation and our decision to leave, my supervisor's response was measured but caring. I'm grateful for his understanding, because the reasons for our departure were personal and painful. We didn't want to leave; we felt we had to. And he sought to comfort us in our difficult choice. But then, at a pivotal point in the conversation, he shared something that, in my grief, was no consolation. It lingers with me to this day: "I've been in this country for a long time," he reflected, "but I've never really seen a church planted and sustained long-term without the involvement of a strong national partner."

His words hit a nerve. Years earlier we'd left another city within the same country to come to this more remote region. At the time, we felt compelled to move. The sheer numbers called us. Statistically, this was the least-reached place we could find on the map. But beyond personal calculations, our organization's leadership was urging us to push eastward and northward into a territory unengaged by other missionaries. No one else was going. Would we answer the call?

But there was one problem: no local believer was ready or willing to come with us. In fact, whenever we shared our vision to go to this unreached and religiously conservative region, most of the national believers cautioned against it. "It's dangerous there; are you sure?" "We'd never consider going there." "Why wouldn't you just stay here and help us?"

What is a missionary to do in such a situation? How would you respond? At the time, I was convinced that the courageous and faithful response—what a pioneer missionary like Paul would do—was to go. The urgent need of the hour was for someone to storm the gates of hell, with or without an accompanying army. Waiting wasn't an option. What if we could never convince a national to join our team? Should we just delay our mission indefinitely?

Perhaps it goes without saying, but Americans don't do well with delays. We live in an age of two-day delivery, when you can receive just about any essential (or nonessential) item at your doorstep within forty-eight hours. If you're ordering milk or cookies, it might only be a matter of minutes. Western Christians also come from a more task-driven and time-conscious culture. Relationships and partnerships, while valued, aren't primary. Maybe most significant of all, few of us operate with a long-term vision. Prudence and patience are social virtues of the past. Our consumeristic culture has given rise to throwaway culture. We value novelty and immediacy more than durability.

This phenomenon might be most obvious in modern architecture. What we build today is gone tomorrow. We don't construct edifices that remain and survive. Gone are the days of cathedrals and castles. Instead, we erect shopping malls and shanties that, within our lifetime, will flatten by wind or by wrecking ball. The same could be said of Christian missions. It would be foolish to assume that our prevailing cultural atmosphere doesn't in some way influence the way we envision overseas ministry.

In missions, we recruit missionaries with urgency, not toward longevity. We tend to go fast, or we don't go at all. We invest untold material and personnel resources to help others in the short term but do so in ways that often hurt them in the long run. We start countless programs and projects, only to watch many fizzle out and die. While our missionary mantra of late has been "Work yourself out of a job," one has to wonder if a more appropriate goal would be, "Build something that lasts."

"Mission Accomplished": The Infamous Words of Western Confidence

In spring 2003, thirty miles off the coast of California on waters gently rippled like gray slate, the crew aboard the USS *Abraham Lincoln* were making final preparations for the arrival of the sitting

American president. The sun's light diffused through a skin of high clouds over the calm Pacific. Halfway around the world it wasn't nearly as serene. The United States was engaged in an intense conflict with the country of Iraq—for exactly six weeks.

I remember sitting in front of the television that March watching the "shock and awe" campaign designed to swiftly bring Saddam Hussein to his knees and eliminate the supposed threat of WMDs. As we watched the fighting unfold from the comfort of our couches, many Americans were relieved to see that the initial surge of the U.S.-led coalition was overwhelmingly successful. In a matter of days, the mission objectives of our allies were being accomplished. By May 1, President George W. Bush was prepared to make a statement to the nation about the state of the war, and he chose the deck of the *Lincoln* as a symbolic stage for his historic address.

But that speech soon became one of the most infamous and ironic moments of recent American history. In it, President Bush declared that major operations in Iraq had ended and the United States, along with her allies, had prevailed. While his words did offer some cautions about the difficult road ahead, the pomp and circumstance of the event conveyed a mood of triumphalism. Americans with a sense of the past couldn't help but equate it with Douglas MacArthur's postwar victory speech aboard the USS *Missouri*. However, as we know, the U.S. involvement in Iraq—including significant escalation in the region with the subsequent advent of ISIS—has continued to this day, making a mockery of American overconfidence in her Mideast campaign. Emblematic of that naïve self-assuredness is the massive banner that was draped astride the *Lincoln* in preparation for the president's arrival, emblazoned with the words: "Mission Accomplished."

If there's one thing history should teach us, it's that commitments to speed and blind self-confidence rarely combine to produce appreciable results. But one of the curious dynamics of Western culture is the odd marriage of these competing characteristics. On the one hand, we like to live in the moment; we prefer to do things fast. On the other, we seem to have incredible confidence in ourselves and the staying power of our efforts. In my experience, these characteristics also shape much of our missionary enterprise.

My concern, and one reason for writing this book, is that we're living at a time in global missions today when the gospel and faithful ministry are threatened by the tyranny of the urgent. We're driven by a vision of "Mission Accomplished." To that end, we've often sacrificed the important for the immediate, the best for the most pressing. Over the last few decades, as our focus has been on reaching the unreached and finishing the task, we've increasingly prioritized rapid reproduction, with a programmatic and results-driven focus that looks more like Western capitalism and business franchising than genuine Christlike servanthood and faithful stewardship.[7]

Democratization of Missions

We live in a day of what could be called the democratization of missions. Everyone is a missionary, and everything we do is mission. As the world continues to shrink, our opportunities keep expanding. But in such a situation, how do we prioritize our limited resources? How does a church know whom to support or where to go? And how can we determine if what we're doing is faithful to Christ's gospel and our mandate?

---

7   See Lesslie Newbigin, *The Open Secret: An Introduction to the Theology of Mission* (Grand Rapids, MI: Eerdmans, 1995), 124–28.

It's not enough to just *do something*. In this hour, one temptation for the church is to respond to the urgent global need by simply trying our best while aiming at the nebulous goal of God's glory. Even if we don't know whether we're effecting change or doing lasting good, we might at least find solace with the impossibility of our task, the nobility of our intentions, and the sovereignty of our God. When our efforts collapse and no legacy survives, we might surrender to the words of the psalmist, "Unless the Lord builds the house, / those who build it labor in vain" (Ps. 127:1).

Don't misunderstand me. The need for building is undoubtedly urgent; the task before us is truly unfinished. So I resonate with voices that call for immediate action. I also appreciate the emphasis on glorifying God and an accompanying God-centered confidence that totally depends on him for success. But there's a wrong way to rest in God's sovereignty while taking great risk. If we steward Christ's gospel and the church's resources yet end up with nothing to show for it, God is not honored. Nor will we be.

Jesus taught that the honorific commendation "Well done, good and faithful servant" is reserved for those who spend wisely, who produce a return on God's investment (Matt. 25:14–30). Paul says much the same, though using the metaphor of construction. Only those who build with the right materials can expect a recompense for their labor: "If the work that anyone has built on the foundation survives, he will receive a reward. If anyone's work is burned up, he will suffer loss" (1 Cor. 3:14–15).

In 1 Corinthians, as in many places throughout the Corinthian correspondence, Paul reveals how God's judgment was a controlling influence over his mission—as it should be over all our missions. What matters on the last day is God's approval of our work and the lasting value of our efforts.[8] Of course, Paul wasn't talking about the structural integrity or legacy of a brick-and-mortar structure in Kampala or Chattanooga. He was suggesting that our reward as ministers of the gospel is directly tied to the quality of our labors. Shoddy work will not be praised.

Today, I'm deeply concerned that much of evangelical Christian missions is a straw house built on a sandy shore. Some of the stories that I'll share throughout this book will reveal as much. From my years living in Asia to my current travels around the globe, what I find are missionaries and ministries with the unbiblical view that, when it comes to missions, any effort is commendable. Equally troubling, many assume that the all-important goal of reaching the lost validates our use of almost any means.

My purpose in this book isn't to criticize or unhelpfully shame; rather, I'm compelled to recount these stories and raise the caution flag—perhaps we need to slow down if danger is around the bend. I also want to call us to another goal, a different end. At such a time as this, we don't necessarily need more impassioned pleas about opportunity and urgency. While those are important, I'm convinced that what we desperately need are voices of discernment, calls for wise investment, and plans for better building.

This book will not answer all our missiological questions, but it will seek to reframe the discussion and reshape our desires by reconsidering the life of Paul. As we observe a more well-textured

---

8   As D. A. Carson writes, "Paul understands that what ultimately matters is whether or not we gain the Lord's approval . . . what matters most in God's universe is what God thinks of us, whether we are approved by him." See D. A. Carson, *A Model of Christian Maturity: An Exposition of 2 Corinthians 10–13* (Grand Rapids, MI: Baker, 2019), 103.

portrait of the apostle and his ministry, we'll find that he often describes the goal of his life in terms of seeking God's approval. The quest for God's praise is what guided Paul's missionary ambition and directed his missionary method.

God's Approval: The End That Guides Our Means

Books about missions tend to focus on either means or ends. Even though they discuss both, inevitably their content is tilted in one direction or the other. Some explore the great purposes of our calling, such as the salvation of the lost, the blessing of God for all nations, and the worship of God from all peoples. Other resources examine missionary methods, such as cross-cultural communication, ministries of mercy, evangelism and discipleship, urban strategies, and church planting—to name only a few.

There is also a formidable tradition of Christian literature that considers the person and ministry of the apostle Paul. Those resources tend to look at his life as exemplary, presenting Paul as the model missionary. As such, they investigate his theology and motivation as well as his strategy and method. The assumption in many cases is that Paul's ambition and approach are at least somewhat normative for Christian missions today.[9]

But what I've found is that we rarely reflect at length on one of the explicit and often repeated goals of Paul: his desire for God's affirmation.[10] Subsequently, we've rarely considered how this over-

---

9   This assumption has been challenged in recent years. See David J. Bosch, *Transforming Mission* (Maryknoll, NY: Orbis Books, 1997). On the validity and necessity of following Paul, see Roland Allen, *Missionary Methods: St. Paul's or Ours?* (Grand Rapids, MI: Eerdmans, 1962). Contra Bosch, see also Peter J. O'Brien, *Gospel and Mission in the Writings of Paul* (Grand Rapids, MI: Baker, 1995), 83–107.

10   As one example, see Eckhard J. Schnabel, "Paul the Missionary," in *Paul's Missionary Methods*, eds. Robert L. Plummer and John Mark Terry (Downers Grove, IL: IVP, 2012), 33.

arching motivation for honor and recognition on the last day had a significant role to play in guiding Paul's missionary approach.

Paul expresses this goal in numerous ways, whether attaining commendation (1 Cor. 4:5; 2 Cor. 10:18) or avoiding disqualification (1 Cor. 9:27), seeking a reward (1 Cor. 3:14; 9:17) or a weight of glory (2 Cor. 4:17), having reason to boast in his sacrifice (1 Cor. 9:15), and even expecting others to boast of him before Christ (2 Cor. 1:14). Whenever we see Paul talk this way, we also find him discussing how his keen awareness of the final judgment was a kind of internal compass that consistently led him in the appropriate direction—on practical issues such as contextualization, partnerships, and giving. As we wrestle with the question of how to do missions like Paul, we'll understand how often we ignore one of the key components to his wisdom and effectiveness.[11]

Of course, as soon as we talk about pleasing God, earning a reward, and receiving God's praise, we're entering murky waters that many evangelicals would rather avoid. We're theologically committed to justification by grace alone through faith alone in Christ alone. Any mention of meritorious labor sounds like works-righteousness that inevitably leads to arrogance—which we know doesn't result in our justification (Luke 18:9–14). We're also committed to living for God's glory alone. We cross the seas with the gospel because God deserves the praise of all nations.[12] Therefore,

---

11 As David Bosch quotes from Paul Minear: "One aim of missiology is a more adequate understanding of the apostolic task of the Church. One aim of exegetical theology is a more adequate understanding of the mind of the biblical writer. When, therefore, the exegete deals with the apostle Paul, and when missiology accepts Paul's apostolic work as normative for the continuing mission of the Church, then these two aims coalesce." See Bosch, *Transforming Mission*, 170.

12 This was the thrust of John Piper's influential book, *Let the Nations Be Glad: The Supremacy of God in Missions* (Grand Rapids, MI: Baker, 1993).

doing missions in view of one day receiving honor from God seems sacrilegious. Such self-seeking is antithetical to the altruistic motives which we assume are superior.[13]

But we evangelicals also base our faith on Scripture alone. And here is where the biblical witness reveals some of our theological and cultural blind spots. For one, Paul was deeply influenced by the theological concept of divine judgment and reward—including qualitative levels of each—just as Jesus taught. In Luke's Gospel alone there are over forty promises of reward or warnings of judgment based on an individual's works. Specifically related to money, Jesus promised a great reward in the kingdom for those who do good and lend to their enemies (Luke 6:35). He promised "moneybags" in heaven for those who give to the needy on earth (Luke 12:33). And he promised a repayment at the resurrection for hospitality toward the poor (Luke 14:14). A central component of Jesus's ethical teaching included motivating his disciples through the opportunity for future rewards.

Paul also lived in a culture that esteemed honor and despised shame. In Corinth, and throughout the Greco-Roman world, many everyday decisions revolved around the pursuit of reputation and reward.[14] But rather than outright reject such self-interest as sinful, Paul redirects it. Like Jesus before him, he calls us to seek glory from God rather than from others (John 5:44). In fact, this motivation exerted significant influence over Paul's missionary ethos, knowing

---

13 For an example of this assumption and the preference for altruism in missions, see David Joannes, *The Mind of a Missionary* (Prescott, AZ: Within Reach Global, 2018).

14 "Corinth was a city where public boasting and self-promotion had become an art form. The Corinthian people thus lived with an honor-shame cultural orientation. . . . In such a culture a person's sense of worth is based on recognition by others of one's accomplishments." See Ben Witherington, *Conflict and Community in Corinth: A Socio-Rhetorical Commentary on 1 and 2 Corinthians* (Grand Rapids, MI: Eerdmans, 1995), 8.

that greater glory was reserved for those who suffered well, humbly served, and faithfully stewarded the gospel.

As a young person, I was always fascinated by Paul. At some point during my time studying missions at a small Bible college, the letter of 2 Corinthians captured my attention and imagination. Like no other book in the Bible, this epistle was a window into the passionate—and often anguished—heart of the apostle. It showed what moved him. In it, I saw Paul talking in ways that were extremely personal and vulnerable. As much as he expounded God's glory and the history of redemption, he pleaded with his friends and beloved partners. Here wasn't dispassionate theological reflection or even purely altruistic motivation. Instead, 2 Corinthians showed me a missionary fully invested, what a real person looks like doing real ministry. In 2 Corinthians, Paul speaks candidly. His missionary heart is exposed for all to see (2 Cor. 6:11).

Not surprisingly, then, the first chance I had to preach in a church, I turned to 2 Corinthians, to what had become one of my favorite passages in the Bible:

> Here for the third time I am ready to come to you. And I will not be a burden, for I seek not what is yours but you. For children are not obligated to save up for their parents, but parents for their children. I will most gladly spend and be spent for your souls. If I love you more, am I to be loved less? (2 Cor. 12:14–15)

The few people who heard that sermon over twenty years ago surely have no recollection of what I said, but it's possible they remember my conviction. Whatever was lost in depth and nuance was made up for in passion. I was compelled by the example of Paul, and I did my level best to communicate it to my hearers. I did so by describing Paul's understanding of Christian ministry—genuine Christlike servanthood—based on these two short verses. Like many aspiring preachers, I organized it into three basic points. The ministry of Paul, I argued, was marked by responsibility, sacrifice, and vulnerability.

That last point gripped me. At the time, I had little experiential knowledge of ministry. The rigors and relational pressures of a pastor or missionary had yet to touch me. Yet I couldn't help but be captivated by the vision of a servant of Christ who would willingly—*and gladly*—give his life for others. Not only that, but he would allow their ongoing needs and struggles to drain him personally, to distract him from what he most desired. Paul was willing to be inconvenienced for the sake of the gospel, to spend and be spent for the Corinthians (2 Cor. 12:15). *They* were the reason he left Troas.

The distressing decision to abandon that open door reveals Paul's utmost care for the Corinthians. As he took pains to demonstrate, Paul wasn't just some peddler of the gospel looking for a buck, for converts to his cause, or for more participants in a pyramid scheme stretching across the known world. Paul was deeply and personally concerned for the Corinthians themselves, for their eternal souls. His willingness to change plans didn't betray an unreliable fickleness. Just the opposite. It showed his utter dependability as a father who would do anything for his wayward and weak children.

Today, long after that first sermon, Paul is still my missionary hero. And 2 Corinthians still fascinates and perplexes me. Why would someone who ultimately cares about God's opinion and approval seem to care so much about the approval and opinion of the Corinthians? Why does someone who boasts only in God and his gospel seem to boast in himself and what God has done through him? How is it that faithfulness is the true measure of a steward, yet Paul suggests that his ministry is also validated by its fruitfulness? These are only a few of my questions. In a way, this book is an excuse for me to think more deeply about them, to reflect on Paul's complex life and ministry, and to meditate on his transparent yet enigmatic correspondence with the Corinthians. But more than my personal musings, I pray this book will serve us all as we consider both the means and ends of our mission. I want us to explore together what faithful gospel ministry looks like when God's approval guides our ambition.

1

Seeking God's Approval

Corinth

SURROUNDED BY HIS railing accusers in the heart of the city's bustling forum, the apostle Paul stood before the Corinthian tribunal, at the imperial judgment seat of Gallio. Paul's crime, according to his Jewish plaintiffs, was that he was persuading others to worship God in ways that contradicted the law of Moses. As the Jewish leaders made their opening arguments before Gallio, Paul prepared his own statement. He would be forced to make a plea to the proconsul of Achaia without the luxury of an attorney.

However, in a strange irony, Paul must have felt a tinge of relief for the opportunity to have his day in court rather than face mob justice. On his first missionary journey, he encountered unruly masses who incited violence against him from Pisidia to Lycaonia. On his second journey, following the call to Macedonia, Paul was beaten and jailed in Philippi. Undeterred, he traveled to Thessalonica and entered the synagogue, reasoning from the Scriptures that it was necessary for the Messiah to suffer. Apparently, suffering was also necessary for

Paul, because the Jews there roused a rabble that "set the city in an uproar" (Acts 17:5), eventually chasing him all the way to Berea.

It shouldn't be surprising, then, that when Paul eventually made his way to Corinth, he came "in weakness and in fear and much trembling" (1 Cor. 2:3). He no doubt still bore the scars, physical and emotional, from multiple beatings. That Paul went straight to the Corinthian synagogue doesn't betray a rugged confidence or bravado as much as an inner compulsion to make Christ known wherever he went.

Still, Paul had to wonder on arrival in Corinth if this would be another abbreviated stop. But as he began to preach Christ crucified—and again face opposition—the Lord appeared to him with a promise of comfort and hope: "Do not be afraid, but go on speaking and do not be silent, for I am with you, and no one will attack you to harm you, for I have many in this city who are my people" (Acts 18:9–10). Instead of fear, Paul was to take courage and continue. Instead of running, he was to remain in Corinth. For the first time in nearly five years, he would put down roots in one place.

But then came his date in court.

Among all the thoughts flooding Paul's mind as he stood before Gallio, he must have rehearsed those reassuring words of Jesus. He recalled that no harm would befall him. But he also remembered that he couldn't stay silent. He was there to bear witness to Christ. However, before Paul could open his lips and make a defense for the hope of Israel—just as he was about to speak—Gallio rendered his verdict. As an internal dispute among Jews about innocuous terminology and their religious practice, his court wouldn't accept the complaint (Acts 18:12–15). Gallio threw out the case.

Whatever relief Paul experienced at that moment was, for him, relatively fleeting and insignificant. Acquittal or condemnation in the eyes of any human court weren't his ultimate concern, because he knew he would one day stand before a far greater Judge, one who would bring everything to light (1 Cor. 4:3–5). Therefore, Paul spent his life, as it were, preparing a statement for the heavenly tribunal. He made it his ambition to receive, on that day, God's commendation.

Avoiding Disqualification

On November 24, 1746, writing from Elizabethtown, New Jersey, missionary David Brainerd penned a letter to his younger brother, Israel, who at the time was a student at Yale. "Dear brother, let me entreat you to keep *eternity* in your view," he urged, "and behave yourself as becomes one that must shortly 'give an account of all things done in the body.'"[1]

At the age of twenty-eight, Brainerd was still well aware of the temptations of youth and university life. He also likely knew his own time was short. Earlier that month he had retired to the house of his friend Jonathan Dickinson. Brainerd's health was deteriorating. He couldn't continue his mission to the Native Americans in New Jersey. Within a few months, he would travel to Massachusetts to be cared for in the home of Jonathan Edwards. Within the year, he would be dead.

As Brainerd composed his counsel to Israel, he echoed Paul's correspondence with the Corinthian church. Specifically, he referenced a passage with much hope for those enduring physical hardship, whose "outer self is wasting away" like a tent in tatters. As Paul writes, "We know that if the tent that is our earthly home is destroyed, we have a building from God, a house not made with

---

1   *The Works of Jonathan Edwards*, vol. 2 (Peabody, MA: Hendrickson, 2006), 437–38.

hands, eternal in the heavens" (2 Cor. 5:1). The hope for Paul the missionary was, as also for Brainerd, that his seemingly endless affliction and suffering would be, one day, "swallowed up by life" (2 Cor. 5:4).

But Paul's overwhelming hope in the resurrection didn't entirely eliminate his fears. Paul was still anxious to receive God's approval on the last day, knowing that he would give an account for everything done "in the body" (2 Cor. 5:10). In fact, this concern fueled in Paul a self-awareness and God-consciousness that guided every step of his ambassadorial ministry. Specifically, as he sought to call others to be reconciled to God, he made it his aim—his ambition—to please God (2 Cor. 5:9).[2] Why? Because he knew that everything he did, whether for good or for ill, would one day be adjudicated at the bar of God. He knew that all people must stand before the judgment seat—not of Gallio, but of Christ.[3] Because of this, on account of the fear of the Lord, Paul spent his life trying to persuade others (2 Cor. 5:10–11).

This awareness was also evident in Paul's missionary method. In a section of 1 Corinthians that highlights how he sought "by all means"[4] to win as many people as possible, we must not miss Paul's complementary concern:

> Do you not know that in a race all the runners run, but only one receives the prize? So run that you may obtain it. Every athlete

2 Paul's goal of pleasing God was also his expectation for those he reached (Eph. 5:10; Col. 1:10; 1 Thess. 4:1).

3 The Greek word *bema* translated in 2 Cor. 5:10 as the "judgment seat" of Christ, is the same used for Gallio's tribunal.

4 Such accommodation can only be "in things indifferent, that are otherwise in our choice" and must not include engaging "in things that the Lord has prohibited." See John Calvin, *Commentary on the Epistles of Paul the Apostle to the Corinthians*, vol. 1 (Grand Rapids, MI: Eerdmans, 1948), 306.

exercises self-control in all things. They do it to receive a perishable wreath, but we an imperishable. So I do not run aimlessly; I do not box as one beating the air. But I discipline my body and keep it under control, lest after preaching to others I myself should be disqualified. (1 Cor. 9:24–27)

Do you see it there in Paul's words? He was concerned for his own disqualification. For Paul, preaching to others without an eye to God's approval would be like running without a sense of direction. It's like entering a race and kicking into the starting blocks without knowledge of the finish line. It's like participating in the Olympic Games and not realizing there are rules and referees. It would be no different, no more useful, than a boxer swinging at air. Aimless.

As Paul made it his ambition to make Christ known among the nations—to reason with them about the coming judgment through the authorized Son of God[5]—he did so cognizant of his own future day before the *bema*. He was aware of his position in the dock. And Paul didn't arrogantly assume that his ministry was sure to receive God's affirmation just because he did it in God's name. As Jesus said, even mighty works accomplished for his sake don't guarantee our acceptance (Matt. 7:21–23). Paul knew that disapproval, even ultimate disqualification, was a real possibility.[6]

---

5 Acts 17:31; 24:25.

6 Don Howell doesn't take Paul's fear of "disqualification" as reason to call into question his assurance of salvation. "Paul is referring not to his final salvation (perhaps implied in AV: 'castaway'), but to the testing of his apostleship. He fears, through the lack of rigorous self-discipline, forfeiting the divine approval through failure to fulfill his apostolic commission as faithful steward of the gospel to the Gentiles." See Don N. Howell Jr., "Paul's Theology of Suffering," in *Paul's Missionary Methods*, eds. Robert L. Plummer and John Mark Terry (Downers Grove, IL: IVP, 2012), 103. For a contrasting position that understands final salvation to be in view, see Thomas R. Schreiner and Ardel B. Caneday, *The Race Set Before Us: A Biblical Theology of Perseverance and Assurance* (Downers Grove,

This should rouse us from any slumbering self-confidence and raise the stakes for our missionary calling. Pursuing the salvation of the lost and reaching the unreached aren't enough to please God, even if those efforts are well-intentioned and carried out with utmost zeal. We must do so in an appropriate manner. Christ's ambassadors must strive to be approved by God and avoid unnecessary shame (2 Tim. 2:15).

But what leads to God's approval and acceptance? If some of God's workers receive a reward while others suffer loss (1 Cor. 3:14–15), what does that reward look like? And how do we reconcile the hope of glory with the potential for disapproval? We must reckon with the possibility that the offering of our missionary lives to God could, in the end, be unacceptable to him.

Wrong Kind of Acceptance

Shame was a real concern the moment Paul stepped foot into Achaia. Corinth was a cosmopolitan city with a reputation for Roman decadence and Greek sophistry. One powerful cultural dynamic directly related to Paul's mission was the practice of ascribing honor to traveling teachers, orators, and sophist philosophers. The more eloquent the rhetorician, the more he could expect his tribe to increase. Not only that, but skilled speakers received financial remuneration from a loyal and growing audience.[7]

IL: IVP, 2001). I believe 1 Cor. 9:24–27 operates as a hinge in Paul's argument, and the danger he will develop in the subsequent chapter certainly has to do with apostasy (1 Cor. 10:1–12). Importantly, neither interpretation allows us to minimize Paul's sobriety before his Judge.

7 See D. A. Carson, *A Model of Christian Maturity: An Exposition of 2 Corinthians 10–13* (Grand Rapids, MI: Baker, 2019), 33. See also Bruce W. Winter, *Philo and Paul among the Sophists: Alexandrian and Corinthian Responses to a Julio-Claudian Movement* (Grand Rapids, MI: Eerdmans, 2001).

But, of course, Paul didn't stride into town as a polished and charismatic figure poised to launch a global movement. He came disgraced by fresh beatings. This meant that the cultural expectations of Corinth could easily work against him. His physical appearance and observable weakness would be a barrier to the gospel's acceptance.

Or would they? What if, instead, Paul could leverage his rhetorical ability to win a hearing? What if he could get the Corinthians to respond positively to his persuasive preaching? He would then be able to make use of any pseudocelebrity status to win more people. Perhaps he could also take advantage of their willingness to financially subsidize his teaching, propelling him to new fields and greater fruit.

We must pause and acknowledge the genuine conundrum here for Paul. He had been on the run for much of his ministry, persecuted in nearly every place. Rejection and affliction became the norm wherever he went. But not only for Paul. We know that in many cities the believers who associated with him were also inundated with suffering. When he stayed around, it usually spelled trouble. And when Paul left town, the trouble didn't always leave with him. From Antioch to Ephesus to Athens, anyone considering Paul's gospel wouldn't just be confronted with the message of a shamefully crucified Jewish Messiah. They would be counting the cost of believing a bruised and bloodied apostle.

But what if Paul could change that? What if he could take advantage of the cultural milieu of Greek sophistry and present a more, well, *sophisticated* message? What if he could leverage his rhetorical skills to create a following, or at least gain an audience?

On a couple occasions I have had the opportunity to travel to an East Asian city where our ministry provides training to church leaders. During one of those trips, I met with an American missionary acquaintance who stopped by the guesthouse where I was staying. As we settled into the spartan space, he shared with me some of the concerns among his teammates, friends, and colleagues living in a country where you can't easily operate as a missionary. Some worked in secular fields. Some chose to secretly gather. Some shied away from overt evangelism. Many struggled to integrate identity, occupation, and ministry in their daily life. It all sounded familiar.

But then he happily volunteered the solution he had discovered. With the help of some locals, he was operating a non-governmental organization (NGO) that worked on community development projects throughout the region. He was grateful to report how this platform supplied him with legitimacy, served the needs of struggling communities, and provided access for the gospel in unreached areas. It sounded perfect. Villages were gladly opening their doors to the work of his NGO, which ultimately opened the door for the gospel. "It's amazing," he added, "the opportunities you have for evangelism when you bring $50,000 worth of investment into a local community."

I was suddenly bewildered. Perhaps he sensed the surprise and confusion on my face, because he went on to explain further.

Recently, he'd had the opportunity to meet with a municipal official in a remote region, someone he assumed would otherwise never hear the gospel or at least never have an interest in listening to it. But since this missionary's NGO was investing heavily in his village, the official was more than happy to give him his undivided attention. Just imagine what could happen, this missionary suggested, if the leader of that unengaged and unreached community would come to Christ.

When we think of the challenges that missionaries face, we often think of persecution. We envision the places they go where the price of following Jesus is the primary reason many hesitate to embrace Christ. Of course, such people and places exist. But there's another, perhaps more sinister—and perhaps more pervasive—challenge that Western missionaries face when they take the gospel to new regions. It's the connection of Christianity to prosperity, status, and glory. The great difficulty for workers in such fields isn't only the fear of loss that makes people reject the gospel; it's also the hope of gain that makes them willing to accept it.[8]

Seeking Honor from God Alone

I'm not sure missionaries are always aware of the trap of seeking others' approval, especially when it feels good to have them accept your message and when it appears strategic to reach a broader community.[9] But when we read Paul's Corinthian correspondence, we discover that he was extremely careful while working in a culture eager to turn the gospel into an opportunity for upward mobility.

From his first day in Corinth, Paul self-consciously refused to preach in a manner that would draw attention to his eloquence and acumen as he highlighted Christ's ignominious crucifixion (1 Cor. 2:1–2; cf. 1:17).[10] He intentionally avoided baptizing most converts, not wanting to convey that he was calling followers to himself (1 Cor. 1:13–16). Paul also refused to accept money from those who embraced his message in order to make it abundantly

---

8 In some mission fields, the fear of suffering and the hope of prosperity can coexist, creating a challenging environment for ministry.

9 This approach is pervasive in the Western church and easily exported by her missionaries.

10 It's not entirely clear if Paul limited himself in the full exercise of his rhetorical abilities as a matter of strategy or if his speaking abilities were also in some way inferior to his knowledge and writing skills (2 Cor. 11:6). In either case, Paul recognized God's purpose at work in him, as it was in Moses who was "slow of speech" (Ex. 4:10), such that the surpassing power would belong to God and not him (2 Cor. 4:7) and God's strength would be perfected in his weakness (2 Cor. 12:9).

clear that God's grace wasn't a commodity to be acquired or a status to be earned (1 Cor. 9:11–14; cf. 2 Cor. 11:7–9). In fact, we have reason to understand that Paul's trembling and weak entrance into Corinth wasn't merely the result of constant suffering but was part of a strategic approach—*so that* their belief in his message would be owing to the power of God and not his persuasive persona (1 Cor. 2:2–5). Paul wanted to be certain that those who received Christ's gospel did so because of the compelling work of the Spirit through the unadorned preaching of God's word.[11] Nothing else.

While Paul could have spun a message that would appeal to the Corinthians' desires and avoid personal suffering, he didn't do so. Why? Because Paul's pursuit of God's approval ruled out the goal of human praise. The two were mutually exclusive. Paul believed that if he, through his preaching, sought the affirmation of others, it could mean rejection from God. He would no longer be the servant of Christ (Gal. 1:10; 1 Thess. 2:4).

Now, I doubt most missionaries consider praise from people as cracking the top ten dangers in their ministry. Instead, we're generally concerned with risks more obvious and ominous, such as the lack of access to quality medical care, slumping financial support, difficulty maintaining residency, limited educational resources, challenges working with national partners, and disunity among expat workers. All of those—not to mention the possibilities of persecution, disease, political unrest, and natural disasters—combine to fill our minds with what truly threatens our ministry.

But if we granted, for a moment, that receiving God's affirmation is of critical concern and one of the highest motivations for our mission, then wouldn't we consider the antithetical desire for

---

11 See Te-Li Lau, *Defending Shame: Its Formative Power in Paul's Letters* (Grand Rapids, MI: Baker, 2020), 109.

others' approval to be a potential snare for Christian ministers? If the greatest missionary of all time repeatedly found this temptation so hazardous, shouldn't we be alert to its perils?

My concern is that many missionaries today, oblivious to this threat, may be caught unawares when it comes to trying to please others. In many cases, we're in danger of tweaking the gospel to make it more appealing, of tampering with God's word to make it more acceptable. We're in danger of connecting Christ to opportunities for money and employment, to offers of goods and services. We're in danger of promoting belief that doesn't come with a cost, of encouraging a Christ-following that doesn't expect an others-leaving. We're in danger of forfeiting our witness and losing personal integrity for the sake of a business platform, governmental recognition, and long-term presence. We're in danger of confusing Christian service with a comfortable career, of presenting Christianity as the pain-free path of professional missionaries.

These problems and more result from seeking approval from others instead of from God. For Paul, this is the issue that ultimately differentiated him from false apostles.[12] And not just in Corinth. It was the defining characteristic that separated Paul's mission from that of many others. False teachers, he observed, were anxious to please people. They were greedy for selfish gain (Phil. 3:17–19). They were eager to take advantage of their followers. They consistently wanted to make a good showing and avoid suffering (Gal. 6:12). They were glory grabbers.

But—and this is terribly important—the gospel doesn't oppose our pursuit of glory altogether. Instead, Jesus tells us to seek approval, glory, and reward, but to do so from God alone (John 5:44).

---

12 "The crux of the division between Paul and his opponents is the question 'Whose approval do we seek?'" See Carson, *A Model of Christian Maturity*, 103.

In fact, this is one way Paul described what it looks like to be a Christian: to "seek for glory and honor and immortality" on the day of judgment (Rom. 2:6–11, 16).[13] People of such faith are justified and will receive praise from God (Rom. 2:29). They are those who have been chosen by the Father and sanctified by the Spirit in order to obtain glory and honor with the Son (2 Thess. 2:14; cf. 1 Pet. 1:7). This is, as Paul taught the Corinthians, the mysterious wisdom "which God decreed before the ages *for our glory*" (1 Cor. 2:7). God doesn't reject our desire for approval; he redirects it.

What makes Christians different isn't that they never seek glory, but that they seek it from God alone—because he's the one who made our hearts with a glory-sized hole in the beginning.[14]

Weight of Glory

Perhaps the most well-known sermon of C. S. Lewis is "The Weight of Glory," delivered to the Church of St. Mary the Virgin in Oxford on June 8, 1942. Its title comes from Paul's stunning estimation to the Corinthians that our "light momentary affliction is preparing for us an eternal weight of glory" (2 Cor. 4:17). What's perhaps lesser known, however, is how Lewis defines such glory.

His talk opens with a word about unselfishness and self-denial. Lewis suggests that many moderns miss how Jesus motivated us to self-sacrifice *through* our desires. If we somehow think that the highest Christian or missionary virtues are altruistic and unselfish, then, Lewis says, we're borrowing more from Kant and the Stoics than from the Scriptures. Our problem isn't desire itself; it's that our

---

13 Te-Li Lau argues that Paul sought to construct "an alternate [divine] court of opinion" that "relativizes and undermines" the pursuit of human honor and shame. See Lau, *Defending Shame*, 131–35.

14 For an introduction to this topic, see JR Vassar, *Glory Hunger: God, the Gospel, and Our Quest for Something More* (Wheaton, IL: Crossway, 2015).

desires are too weak. He famously illustrates this with the image of an ignorant child contentedly making mud pies in the slums because he's unaware of the opportunity to enjoy sandcastles at the sea. Intentionally or not, Lewis's illustration reveals another problem. It isn't simply that our desires are tepid. It's that we don't always know what we should want. We're blissfully unaware of what could bring us infinite joy. For Lewis, the source of such joy is glory—though not exactly the kind of glory that he first imagined.

When I began to look into this matter I was shocked to find such different Christians as Milton, Johnson, and Thomas Aquinas taking heavenly glory quite frankly in the sense of fame or good report. But not fame conferred by our fellow creatures—fame with God, approval or (I might say) "appreciation" by God. And then, when I had thought it over, I saw that this view was scriptural; nothing can eliminate from the parable of the divine *accolade*, "Well done, thou good and faithful servant." With that, a good deal of what I had been thinking all my life fell down like a house of cards. I suddenly remembered that no one can enter heaven except as a child; and nothing is so obvious in a child—not in a conceited child, but in a good child—as its great and undisguised pleasure in being praised. Not only in a child, either, but even in a dog or a horse. Apparently what I had mistaken for humility had, all these years, prevented me from understanding what is in fact the humblest, the most childlike, the most creaturely of pleasures—nay, the specific pleasure of the inferior: the pleasure of beast before men, of child before its father, a pupil before his teacher, a creature before its Creator.[15]

15 C. S. Lewis, *The Weight of Glory* (New York: HarperCollins, 1980), 36–37.

Lewis had come to understand that glory "means good report with God, acceptance by God, response, acknowledgment, and welcome into the heart of things."[16] This is the glory that we seek: not just giving praise *to* God but receiving praise *from* God. Such honor is tangible, relatable, and desirable. But so often when we talk of glory, or hear it taught, the concept sounds impersonal, unattainable, and irrelevant. To many of us, the joys of heaven are ethereal and the glory of God esoteric. As a result, the Bible's many promises about glory feel disconnected from our greatest desires. But listen to Lewis's logic: our innermost longings point to a world where those desires can be fulfilled. Our hunger for praise from others is a hunger satiated by God himself.

The earthly approval of a boss that lightens our load; the affirmation of a teacher that brightens our day; the recognition of a proud father and the praise of a delighted spouse: these are all shafts of light directing our eye to the fullness of glory that awaits in heaven. Perhaps most shockingly of all, this hope of glory transforms entirely the Christian's perspective of the judgment seat, turning it from a place of dread and shame to a place of honor and rejoicing!

It is written that we shall "stand before" Him, shall appear, shall be inspected. The promise of glory is the promise, almost incredible and only possible by the work of Christ, that some of us, that any

---

16 Lewis, *Weight of Glory*, 41. Lewis outlines five biblical categories of heavenly reward: (1) to be with God, (2) to be like God, (3) to have glory, (4) to feast, and (5) to rule. While he doesn't explore this, each category relates in some way to the concept of glory. For example, (1) honor comes by being closely associated with the King (Job 36:7; 1 Sam. 2:8). (2) Glory is part of what it means to be made like God (1 Cor. 11:7) in his radiance and beauty (Matt. 13:43; Dan. 12:3). (3) To possess glory includes receiving honor and praise from God (Rom. 2:7; 1 Pet. 1:7). (4) Immense honor is communicated in the idea of feasting with the King at his table (Matt. 8:5–13; Luke 14:7–11). (5) Ruling at his side in dominion over creation communicates restored honor for humanity (Ps. 8; 1 Cor. 6:3).

of us who really chooses, shall actually survive that examination, shall find approval, shall please God. To please God . . . to be a real ingredient in the divine happiness . . . to be loved by God, not merely pitied, but delighted in as an artist delights in his work or a father in a son—it seems impossible, a weight or burden of glory which our thoughts can hardly sustain. But so it is.[17]

According to Lewis, we shouldn't shrink in shame at the thought of standing before God. Instead, we should press toward the finish line with anticipation—with the hope of hearing his commendation and receiving the prize. On that day, our God-given desire for approval, acceptance, and affirmation will finally be attained, supplied by God himself.

But the question remains: Is equal affirmation and glory guaranteed to every Christian? Or are there varying rewards in the kingdom?

Differing Weights, Varying Rewards

Thus far we've explored how one of the great ambitions for Paul the missionary was receiving God's affirmation. I've suggested that this pursuit of God's praise motivated his ministry and guided his approach—also directing him away from the approval of others. However, there is one final component necessary to turn this engine into the driving force behind our missionary efforts: *as we seek God's commendation, we can expect varying degrees of reward and differing weights of glory.*

---

17 Lewis, *Weight of Glory*, 38–39. D. A. Carson adds, "How wonderful! The King of the universe, the Sovereign who has endured our endless rebellion and sought us out at the cost of his Son's death, climaxes our redemption by praising us!" See D. A. Carson, *The Cross and Christian Ministry* (Grand Rapids, MI: Baker, 2007), 101.

Of all that I'm saying in this chapter, this may run most counter to our thinking.[18] It might feel unjust that God would grant more honor to some than others. Or perhaps we're concerned that different levels of honor would inevitably lead to division, comparison, and envy. Or maybe we're inclined to think a motivation for personal glory turns missionaries into heartless mercenaries. What about serving to the glory of God?

Before we can attempt to answer those concerns, we should address the more fundamental question, Does the Bible teach varying degrees of reward for the saints? Here, I offer as an answer a brief sketch.[19]

First, we could appeal to the character of God, specifically his impartial justice. Jesus suggests there will be varying degrees of punishment for individuals based on their situation, understanding, and exposure to the truth (Matt. 10:15; 11:20–24). He also indicates that the wicked will be judged in different ways based on their intentions and actions, as well as their influence over others to sin (Matt. 5:22; 12:36–37; 18:5–7; 23:13).[20] This demonstrates that God is impartial and equitable, repaying the wrongdoer according to wrongs done. But if this is the case, we might assume he would repay the labors of believers similarly, commensurate with their work.[21] It would seemingly be unjust to reward all

---

18 Some scholars reject the idea of varying rewards in the kingdom. For an example, see Craig L. Blomberg, "Degrees of Reward in the Kingdom of Heaven," *JETS* 35/2 (June 1992): 159–72. However, while Blomberg opposes any distinctions for believers that persist throughout eternity, he concedes varying measures of reward or shame at the day of judgment based on texts like 1 Cor. 3:11–15 and 1 John 2:28.

19 This summary is primarily based on Matthew's Gospel, though I will develop this theme from the Corinthian correspondence in subsequent chapters.

20 See also Luke 12:47–48; Rom. 2:5; Heb. 10:29; Rev. 18:6–7.

21 Col. 3:22–25 seems to make this logical connection. Slaves should obey their masters, knowing that God rewards righteousness just as he pays back the wrongdoer. Eph. 6:6–8 makes this

believers equally when some have served more diligently and suffered more nobly.[22]

Second, we could argue from the comparative and superlative language Jesus employs to emphasize our reward. Jesus says that those who suffer should rejoice because they can expect a reward that is great (Matt. 5:11–12). Jesus teaches that, in the kingdom, the humble will be the greatest (Matt. 18:1–4). He also encourages faithful service by saying the last will be first (Matt. 19:30; 20:16).[23] When asked to reserve the highest seats of honor for two disciples, Jesus doesn't reject such a distinction but asserts that those positions are prepared by the Father alone (Matt. 20:20–23).

Third, we could reference the principle of sowing and reaping: the harvest gathered corresponds to labor given. In the parable of talents, those who faithfully invested received a return proportionate to their investment (Matt. 25:14–30). Jesus also promises other rewards that directly connect to our service. The one who receives a prophet will receive a prophet's reward; the one who receives a righteous person, their reward, and so forth (Matt. 10:41). Furthermore, this teaching implies that the righteous person and the prophet respectively have a reward unique to their work. Last, in this same passage, Jesus says that the person who gives a cup of cold water to one of his disciples will by no means lose his reward (Matt. 10:42; cf. Prov. 19:17).

---

very claim, promising eschatological reward for the good each one does. See Constantine R. Campbell, *Paul and the Hope of Glory: An Exegetical and Theological Study* (Grand Rapids, MI: Zondervan, 2020), 151–52.

22 Some argue against this from Matt. 20:1–16. However, that parable warns against comparison among disciples by focusing on the generosity of the Master. See also 1 Cor. 3:8; Heb. 6:10; 1 Pet. 1:17.

23 Some suggest that when the last are first and the first last, we are all equal. But in that reading, the logical force of Jesus's statement vanishes. If all rewards are the same, how do they encourage exceptional sacrifice or service?

"But this could not be true," reasons Jonathan Edwards, "if a person should have no greater reward for doing many good works than if he did a few." In fact, Edwards's sermon on Romans 2:10 argues at length that Christians can and should expect varying experiences of joy and honor from God at judgment day:

> There are different degrees of happiness and glory in heaven. As there are degrees among the angels, *viz.* thrones, dominions, principalities, and powers; so there are degrees among the saints. . . . The glory of the saints above will be in some proportion to their eminency in holiness and good works here. Christ will reward all according to their works. He that gained ten pounds was made ruler over ten cities, and he that gained five pounds over five cities (Luke 19:17; 2 Cor. 9:6). "He that soweth sparingly, shall reap sparingly; and he that soweth bountifully shall reap also bountifully." And the apostle Paul tells us that, as one star differs from another star in glory, so also it shall be in the resurrection of the dead (1 Cor. 15:41).[24]

While Edwards clearly affirms a distinction in rewards for believers, he's also keen to show that such differences don't necessitate envy or discontentment. All rewards will result in our shared happiness and praise of God. Furthermore, just as the Spirit dispenses different gifts to the church now, it shouldn't surprise us—or make us question his justice—if God should bestow different levels of glory and authority in the kingdom. Should some receive greater honor, we will all rejoice with them (1 Cor. 12:26).

24 Edwards, *Works*, 902. (Scripture references are updated to comport with citation style.)

But that still leaves us with a crucial question: how does this relate to the Christian's ultimate purpose of doing all to the glory of God (1 Cor. 10:31)? And doesn't this promise of reward turn Christian missions into a mercenary affair? For an answer, it's helpful to return to Lewis. He insists that an act becomes mercenary only when the reward has no *natural connection* with it, such as when a man marries a woman only for her money. But herein lies the beauty of understanding how God's glory is, and has been since creation, *naturally connected* to our glory.

When God formed the world, he made us, male and female, in his image and likeness to demonstrate his glory as representative rulers commissioned to fill the earth (Gen. 1:26–28). Even though this crown of honor for mankind (Ps. 8:5) was tarnished by sin, God's gracious purpose was to restore a clear reflection of his image in humanity. This happened supremely in one man, Jesus Christ, who perfectly revealed God's glory (John 1:14–18; Col. 1:15; Heb. 1:1–4). But redemption remains incomplete until creation is finally liberated from corruption and God's image bearers are fully restored to honor (Rom. 8:18–21). At that time, God's original plan will be realized when his glory fills the earth as his glorified children reign upon it (Num. 14:21; Hab. 2:14).[25] This is what creation groans for even now (Rom. 8:22).

Since the beginning, God has inextricably linked his glory to his people. Therefore, when God's children are glorified and restored to honor, it in no way diminishes his glory but instead increases

---

25 According to Constantine Campbell, the new creation will be "the arena for the glory of the children of God," as the coheirs of Christ reign with him and have God's glory revealed in them such that they "shine throughout the created realm alongside the glory of Christ." See Campbell, *Paul and the Hope of Glory*, 217, 258. See also Robert A. Peterson, "Pictures of Heaven," in *Heaven*, eds. Christopher W. Morgan and Robert A. Peterson (Wheaton, IL: Crossway, 2014), 179–84.

it. Just as Jesus was exalted and given a name above every name, redounding ultimately to the glory of the Father (Phil. 2:5–11), so too, the apostle Paul could expect that any honor he received for his service would translate into greater glory to Christ (Phil. 1:20–26; cf. 2 Thess. 1:10–12).

This, then, is the *natural connection* that removes the threat of a mercenary spirit in our missionary ambition. We pursue praise *from* God in order to render greater praise *to* God. We seek a crown of glory from him that we might joyfully return it at his feet (Rev. 4:4, 10).

Paul's Crown of Boasting

But now we must return to Corinth. For it's there that we see how this perspective of reward and glory steered Paul's missionary method.

Specifically, Paul understood that the Corinthians' reception of his gospel didn't result just in their rescue and God's glory but also in his validation. Paul—the confident apostle who didn't consult with the influential Jerusalem leaders, the one whose appointment and approval was from God alone—felt confirmed in his life's work through the visible, tangible result of the Corinthians' faith. They were, of all things, the seal of his apostleship and his "letter of recommendation" (1 Cor. 9:1–2; 2 Cor. 3:1–3). In a way, Paul's ministry was substantiated by its fruitfulness in Corinth.[26]

But this observable fruit from his Corinthian ministry was more than just a psychological comfort for Paul. His earnest desire was that, on the last day, the Corinthians would boast before the Lord of their apostle, just as he would of them (2 Cor. 1:14; cf. 5:12; 9:3).

---

26 The statement "In ministry, success is measured by faithfulness" doesn't fully or helpfully capture this aspect of Paul's self-assessment. But success is also not measured by mere fruitfulness. Paul could judge according to fruit because he had conducted his ministry faithfully and wisely.

Writing to the Thessalonians, Paul says much the same: "What is our hope or joy or crown of boasting before our Lord Jesus at his coming? Is it not you? For you are our glory and joy" (1 Thess. 2:19–20; cf. Phil. 4:1). Those whom Paul reached for Christ throughout his missionary life became, for him, a cause for glorious rejoicing.

But wait a minute! Isn't such boasting antithetical to the purposes of God? God's design to magnify his own glory—even his plan to eliminate human boasting—seems contradictory to Paul's pursuit of glory and his plan to boast at the judgment seat of Christ. However, we should recognize that while Paul does expect to joyfully boast one day, it's not in anything he's accomplished; he will boast only in what Christ has done through him.[27] All of Paul's boasting is ultimately a boasting "in the Lord" (1 Cor. 1:31).

However—and particularly important for our study—Paul didn't expect to boast in those who merely believed. Nor did he confidently check the box when a city was "reached" or when a church was established. Instead, Paul connected his boasting to the strength, stability, and long-term viability of a congregation. In the case of Corinth, that boast was at risk. This troubled assembly, first with its arrogant divisions and immoral practice, then with its doubting of their apostle and his gospel, called into question his ability to rejoice over them at the coming of Christ.

This is why Paul includes in the description of his apostolic ministry the goal of "winning" the weak—of reaching those already reached (1 Cor. 9:22).[28] Paul is willing to do whatever is necessary to win the Corinthians *completely*, so that they will be prepared

---

27 Rom. 15:17; 1 Cor. 15:10; Gal. 2:8; Eph. 3:7.

28 In the context of 1 Cor. 8–9, Paul is specifically addressing an issue related to weak Christians. This is also evident in Paul's appeal to "you" (the Corinthian church) to be reconciled to God (2 Cor. 5:20).

for the final day.[29] According to Lesslie Newbigin, Paul doesn't define ministry success in terms of conversions or even the rapid numerical growth of his churches. His "primary concern is with their faithfulness, with the integrity of their witness."[30] Paul's great missionary aim is to develop everyone within his spiritual care to full maturity (Col. 1:28–29).[31]

This desire—Paul's goal of presenting everyone mature in Christ—draws on the metaphor of a priestly offering. Paul's service to Christ isn't just the sacrifice of his own life to the glory of God and in order to reach others (Phil. 2:17; 2 Tim. 4:6). He also wants, in the fruit of his missionary labors, a pleasing and acceptable offering to bring before the Lord on the last day. According to his letter to the Romans, Paul's apostolic calling is "to be a minister of Christ Jesus to the Gentiles in the high priestly service of the gospel of God." His purpose in this is "that the offering of the Gentiles may be *acceptable, sanctified by the Holy Spirit*" (Rom. 15:16; cf. 1:5). When this happens, in Paul's words, he has "*reason to be proud of my work* for God" (Rom. 15:17).

This is a striking revelation from, of all places, Romans 15. In the paradigmatic passage on Paul's great ambition to reach the unreached (Rom. 15:20), we see that he is concerned with more than just new frontiers. Paul desires to rejoice in what Christ has accomplished through him (Rom. 15:18). And what makes his priestly offering acceptable is that those in his influence are living

---

29 "Nothing short of this will fulfil Paul's ambitions for them." See Peter J. O'Brien, *Gospel and Mission in the Writings of Paul* (Grand Rapids, MI: Baker, 1995), 95.

30 Lesslie Newbigin, *The Open Secret: An Introduction to the Theology of Mission* (Grand Rapids, MI: Eerdmans, 1995), 125–26.

31 "Paul energetically labored not to gain large numbers of converts but to present each person mature in Christ." See Don Howell, as quoted by David J. Hesselgrave, *Paradigms in Conflict: 10 Key Questions in Christian Missions Today* (Grand Rapids, MI: Kregel, 2005), 154.

in a manner worthy of the gospel, mature in Christ, sanctified by the Spirit, and obedient in faith. Paul's ability to boast on the last day is connected to the fruit of his labors. According to F. F. Bruce, "When the time came, he was sure that the Lord's adjudication would depend on the quality of his converts."[32]

Years ago, while still living in Central Asia, I was introduced to a man in my city who was somewhat interested in Christianity. He had previously come into contact with a church five hours away. Before our family moved to the region, this church had sent representatives on occasion to meet with him and others who had questions about the Bible. Now that I lived in his hometown, I had taken some responsibility in following up with him.

One day, he asked if we could talk, so I set up a meeting at my friend's office in the evening. The man arrived distraught. He was in a rough spot: out of work, addicted to sin, hopeless. As he exposed his heartache, I tried to encourage him with the good news of Jesus. When he expressed fear about possible persecution, I carefully asked him to count the cost. That night, after much discussion, he cried out to God in tears for mercy and deliverance.

Then, just as we were about to leave the office, he asked if I could help him buy a twenty-dollar one-way bus ticket to get him to the church five hours away. He wanted to share with them what God had done for him. Since they were having a Bible conference that week, it seemed like perfect timing. I gladly handed him the cash and sent him on his way. A few days afterward, though, I heard word from the church. "Please don't do that again," they cautioned. "It sends all the wrong signals." Perhaps not surprisingly, I never heard from the man again.

---

32 F. F. Bruce, *1 & 2 Thessalonians* (Waco: Word, 1982), 56.

What that simple experience demonstrates is that Western missionaries must be extremely careful about connecting the gospel to people's aspirations for a better life. Whether it's pocket cash, a job, or a large investment into community development, we cannot afford to confuse the gospel of Jesus with Western power, influence, status, and prosperity. It's like dumping excess fertilizer on a sprouting lawn in the spring. It might quickly green, but by summer it's burnt brown.

The goal of missions isn't quick gains but lasting results. We must constantly remind ourselves of this, because, like Paul, we want to have an acceptable offering to present before God on the last day.

Heavenly Tribunal

Perhaps it goes without saying in a book on missions, but all authority in heaven and earth has been given to Jesus. That includes the authority to send and to save. It also includes the prerogative to judge[33]—not just the wicked and the sinner, but the works of each of us, his servants. The risen Christ has full jurisdiction throughout the cosmos, and he will preside one day in judgment over all creation. At that time, he will render to each person according to his or her deeds.

Even as Paul was fully confident of his acceptance before God through faith in Jesus, every step of his apostolic ministry was directed by the vision of one day standing before the heavenly tribunal. However, I'm convinced that Paul didn't do so filled with anxiety and dread. His thoughts about approaching the bench— Christ's *bema* seat—weren't consumed by fear. He wasn't anticipat-

33 Matt. 16:27; John 5:22, 27.

ing shame, failure, and ultimate disqualification (2 Tim. 4:6–8). He was preparing for glory.

But that confidence was directly connected to the way Paul had conducted his ministry. If he had cut corners or worked for people's praise, it would have resulted in shame and loss. This means that we too, as missionaries, should carefully consider every aspect of our ministries. Not all sacrifices receive God's acceptance. Divine commendation is not the birthright of every missionary. As Paul writes, "It is not the one who commends himself who is approved, but the one whom the Lord commends" (2 Cor. 10:18). One day, all that we have ever done will be brought to light. At that time, good and faithful servants will receive their praise from God (1 Cor. 4:5).

2

Suffering with Christ

Damascus

INTO A BASKET MADE OF braided rope Saul slumped, knees pulled to his chest, as his palms clung to coarse strands that smelled of fish and the sea. Slowly he sank, first through a wall, then down its rocky ledge. He was lowered. In a deliberate and tenuous fall, he dangled toward the unseen, squinting at shadows in the darkness. Finally, at the feeling of firm ground and slack rope, he scurried to untangle himself from the clinging cords. Saul was free—at least as free as a man on the run could be. He had escaped from Damascus undetected.

Since his life-altering vision on the road to Syria, Saul had been reasoning in the synagogues of Damascus and confounding the Jewish leaders by demonstrating that Jesus of Nazareth was in fact Messiah. As a result, many among them were incensed at his preaching. But Saul hadn't remained only in Damascus. He had soon pressed into the region of the Nabateans to the south and east, into Arabia. From his initial call, Saul knew that he had been apprehended by the Lord for a specific purpose. He wouldn't preach just to Jews. He was to be the apostle to the Gentiles (Acts 9:15). Apparently in his travels throughout Arabia, Saul was exactly that. In a matter of months he had become something of a thorn in the side of Aretas, king of the Nabateans.[1]

After some time, though, Saul found himself back in Damascus. But his return wasn't welcome. The Jews hatched a plot to kill him, stationing sentries at the city gates. Meanwhile, the local governor, under the direction of King Aretas—and likely in league with Jewish authorities—also had guards on duty with direct orders to arrest Saul. The dragnet was closing. After a time, it became clear to Saul and the other disciples that his only way out was the way down.

Could a departure be more different than its arrival?

Some two years prior, Saul approached Damascus from the south, striding up the main thoroughfare under the noonday sun. He came with a mandate, carrying letters from Caiaphas, the high priest. Just as Saul had done in Judea, his mission in Syria was to round up followers of the Way and deliver them, bound to Jerusalem. Luke tells us that Saul came to Damascus intent to kill. But he left running for his life. He came the persecutor but left the persecuted. He came breathing threats but left gasping for air. He came with honor, authority, and power. He left in weakness, chased by rulers and religious authorities, lowered in a basket.

This is how Paul, many years later, remembered that night. When his beloved church in Corinth, influenced by arrogant false teachers—themselves with foreign letters of recommendation—wanted Paul to present his credentials and boast of his accomplishments,

---

1 Eckhard J. Schnabel, *Paul the Missionary* (Downers Grove, IL: IVP, 2008), 60–65. Martin Hengel surmises that for Paul these initial years in Damascus and Arabia "must have been of foundational importance." See Martin Hengel, "Paul in Arabia," *Bulletin for Biblical Research* 12.1, (2002): 65.

Paul provided the details of his trip down the wall. "If I must boast," he conceded, "I will boast of the things that show my weakness" (2 Cor. 11:30). Pushed to the edge by those who demanded a sign, Paul spoke of his shame. He knew that he wasn't appointed just to bear witness to Christ among the nations. He was also called to suffer (Acts 9:16). Paul's many afflictions, rather than discredit his ministry or discourage the missionary, served to confirm his calling and invigorate him with comfort.

Things as They Are

Writing from her home in Dohnavur in 1903, Irish missionary and prolific author Amy Carmichael composed what was to become her most recognized work, *Things as They Are: Mission Work in Southern India*. From her earliest days in cross-cultural ministry, Carmichael was prone to disregard the Victorian sensibilities of her time when it came to missionary reporting. Elisabeth Elliot, in her biography of Carmichael, notes how she consistently told the truth as she saw it.

> She turned with an instinctive deadly nausea from any coloring of the facts, any slightest bending of the truth in order to create a more interesting picture. She was far ahead of her time as a missionary reporter. The constituency was accustomed to a certain triumphalism in missionary stories. Not that there were none like Amy who told it straight, but there were many who popularized mission work by dramatizing the successes and skipping lightly over what was far more commonplace than success. "There isn't much of a halo in real life," she wrote, "we save it all up for the missionary meetings."[2]

2 Elisabeth Elliot, *A Chance to Die: The Life and Legacy of Amy Carmichael* (Grand Rapids, MI: Revell, 2005), 105–6.

This was Carmichael's conviction from earliest days. Writing many years earlier from Japan, her first overseas assignment, Amy summarized her thoughts to supporters: "Throw a love-halo round us, as shining as ever you like, but don't, if you wish to be true, adorn us with one more romantic."[3]

For Carmichael, "things as they are" included the mundane of life, the total lack of privacy, strange foods, and the general loss of creature comforts (though she still managed the occasional pleasure of a British teatime). But, most pressingly, she spoke with stark candor about the challenges of ministry, including language barriers, disinterested hearers, and fruitless labors. She also pulled back the curtain on the reality of emotional anguish, the piercing loneliness of being a single missionary, sickness, corruption, and the dreadful effects of idolatry and sexual exploitation.

But Amy Carmichael didn't record her struggles as a kind of holy grumbling. Nor was she pleading for sympathy. She simply thought people back home should know the truth. And she preferred to recruit new workers to the field with realism rather than romanticism. She didn't want missionary applicants who fancied an exciting adventure or even dreamed of a worthy cause. She expected candidates who "truly desire to live a crucified life." As she stated bluntly, "Do not come unless you can say to your Lord and to us, *The Cross is the attraction*."[4]

If anyone knew the crucified life, it must have been Paul (2 Cor. 4:10–11). He lived with constant threats and ever-present anxiety. In the course of his ministry, he experienced numerous imprison-

---

3 Elliot, *Chance to Die*, 77.

4 This policy arose from the issue of many who had come but failed to stay. "The crucified life did not look quite the same to them in Dohnavur as it had looked on paper." See Elliot, *Chance to Die*, 265.

ments, multiple lashings, countless beatings, and was often near death. At least once he was stoned. He logged innumerable miles on foot across rugged, mountainous terrain, sometimes carrying large sums of money.[5] He was in constant danger by robbers. Crisscrossing journeys on the Mediterranean brought other risks; four times he survived shipwreck.[6] He also endured cold and exposure, hunger and thirst, passing many a night without sleep.[7] Perhaps worst of all, Paul knew the heartache, like his Savior, of being abandoned and betrayed by his friends (2 Cor. 11:23–28).

As Amy Carmichael had come to understand, the way of the cross is the winnowing of missionaries.

But even though Paul withstood the test, his sufferings ultimately separated him from those who should have been his greatest supporters—those meant to hold the ropes.[8] In particular, the Corinthians had come to prefer an apostle who represented their personal aspirations for the good life (1 Cor. 4:8–13). Influenced by false teachers and a society obsessed with personal achievement, abundant prosperity, and glorious power, they struggled to see glory in weakness, especially if that weakness was in their leader.[9]

---

5   Eckhard Schnabel estimates that Paul traveled a total of fifteen thousand miles as a missionary, nearly nine thousand of which by land. See Schnabel, *Paul the Missionary*, 122.

6   The three shipwrecks recorded in 2 Corinthians were all before the event Luke records in Acts 27.

7   Paul, who elsewhere wrote that God supplies all our needs, knew what it was to be without necessary food and clothing (Phil. 4:10–13, 19).

8   William Carey is known for his willingness "to go down" to India provided others, such as Andrew Fuller, would "hold the ropes." No doubt, the apostle Paul's pain was compounded by the Corinthians' embarrassment toward his afflictions and unwillingness to hold tightly to their partnership.

9   In an honor-shame culture, the expectation is for good leaders to "win honor to share it with others." See Jackson W., *Reading Romans with Eastern Eyes: Honor and Shame in Paul's Message and Mission* (Downers Grove, IL: IVP, 2019), 18. However, Paul accepted shame and suffering as the means to bring the Corinthians to glory.

So, when they received word from Paul's missionary travels, either by letter or by representative, they weren't necessarily inspired or impressed by tales of distress, affliction, and shame. Instead, those reports led to greater misgivings about Paul's authority and approach. The Corinthians had accepted the word of the cross, but the way of the cross still seemed a little foolish.

Facing this challenge—a church with a less-than-favorable assessment of his ministry—Paul didn't hold back in his reporting. He refused to sugarcoat stories or selectively describe his missionary successes. Rather, he seemed to do just the opposite. Throughout the Corinthian correspondence, Paul unleashed the full force of his many trials, hardships, and problems, sometimes doing so with stinging sarcasm (1 Cor. 4:10).

Paul desired total transparency in the audit of his gospel ministry. He didn't do this to exaggerate his troubles, to brag about sufferings, or to procure their benevolence. He was simply telling things as they are. He wanted his children in the faith to understand what it looks like to share in Christ's afflictions and in his comfort. He wanted them to understand that his sufferings—contrary to their opinion—authenticated his apostleship and his gospel. To be an ambassador in the kingdom is to bear the marks of the crucified King. But as we share in his sufferings, we also share in his glory.

Sharing in Christ's Afflictions and Comfort

"We do not want you to be unaware," Paul reveals, "of the affliction we experienced in Asia. For we were so utterly burdened beyond our strength that we despaired of life itself. Indeed, we felt that we had received the sentence of death" (2 Cor. 1:8–9). For the Corinthians, it was likely hard to swallow such a raw revelation of Paul's personal angst. But he felt the need to describe for them, with unrelenting honesty, his dreadful experiences in Ephesus. He had been crushed under the enormous weight of suffering.

But this undiluted disclosure of weakness makes Paul's perspective of God's grace all the more astonishing. Only a few lines earlier, just after the opening salutation, Paul praises God as "the Father of mercies and God of all comfort, who comforts us *in all* our affliction" (2 Cor. 1:3–4).

Such comfort isn't necessarily escape *from* injury or even relief *from* pain. This isn't the feeling you get when you're finally debt free or the cancer is gone. It's not the warmth of sunshine after the clouds of trouble have passed by. Instead, this consolation is what God provides *during* the trials and turbulence of life. He is our refuge and strength, a help that's present *within* our times of need (Ps. 46:1).

Therefore, Paul could be content in every situation, seeing the good *in all* his suffering: "We are afflicted in every way, but not crushed; perplexed, but not driven to despair; persecuted, but not forsaken; struck down, but not destroyed" (2 Cor. 4:8–9). This is also the lesson of Paul's stinging thorn in the flesh: that God's strength is perfected *in* our weakness (2 Cor. 12:9). Paul the missionary understands that God's power is magnified when it's residing *within* jars of clay.

But that power also works *through* us in our times of trouble (2 Cor. 6:8–10). Specifically, Paul was consoled by the knowledge that God was at work *through* his missionary dying. His suffering for the sake of the gospel was instrumental in bringing eternal life to the nations.[10] "If we are afflicted," he writes, "it is for your comfort and salvation" (2 Cor. 1:6). Even as death was having its

---

10 Paul even viewed his imprisonments as contributing to the spread of the gospel (Eph. 3:1; Phil. 1:12–14; 2 Tim. 2:9; cf. Acts 28:30–31). "The advance of Paul's mission, that is, the

way with Paul, new life was extending to others (2 Cor. 4:12). This is part of what it means to share in Christ's sufferings as well as his comfort.[11]

However, as we have seen, the afflictions Paul experienced weren't limited to persecution, physical pain, or natural calamities, as excruciating as those must have been. And his sufferings didn't involve just the pioneer advance of the gospel to new peoples, as important as that was. For Paul, sharing in Christ's sufferings also included his care for newly established and existing congregations (2 Cor. 11:28).[12] In fact, when Paul talked about his afflictions, this is one specific kind of suffering he had in mind.

For example, on his initial missionary push into Macedonia, persecution forced Paul to leave the new believers at Thessalonica. He then proceeded southward toward Berea and on to Athens. While there, Paul worried for the welfare of the Thessalonian church. He had left sooner than he wanted. And now Satan hindered him from returning. But Paul also knew that the Thessalonians were themselves facing a trial of hardship. When he could no longer bear the thought of their separation, Paul commissioned Timothy to travel back to Macedonia to encourage the church. Later, Timothy returned with the good news of their steadfast faith and love—and their enduring commitment to their apostle. Paul was greatly relieved. As a result, he tells the Thessalonians that "in all

---

progress of the gospel occurred through his suffering." See Thomas R. Schreiner, *Paul: Apostle of God's Glory in Christ* (Downers Grove, IL: IVP, 2001), 99.

11 Heb. 12:2. As Barnett observes, salvation comes uniquely through the death and resurrection of Christ. But the Corinthians' salvation was also realized through the afflictions of Paul for their sake. Sadly, "what they tend to despise in him is part and parcel of what brought life to them." See Paul Barnett, *The Second Epistle to the Corinthians* (Grand Rapids, MI: Eerdmans, 1997), 77.

12 Paul called Timothy to share in the sufferings of Christ through his long-term role at the church at Ephesus (2 Tim. 1:8; 2:3).

our distress and *affliction* we have been *comforted* about you through your faith" (1 Thess. 3:7).[13]

This same dynamic was present in Corinth as well. When Paul composed the opening lines of 2 Corinthians about the comfort of God in all his afflictions, he was reflecting on what initially pulled him away from the open door in Troas.[14] The afflictions Paul had in mind weren't just the deadly peril in Asia Minor. They also included his anxiety and anguish that the Corinthians were being led astray by arrogant teachers and triumphalist theology (2 Cor. 2:4). Thus, the comfort that he desired—and the comfort God provided—was to see the Corinthians demonstrate genuine faith and willing obedience to Titus.

> For even when we came into Macedonia, our bodies had no rest, but we were afflicted at every turn—fighting without and fear within. But God, who comforts the downcast, comforted us by the coming of Titus, and not only by his coming but also by the comfort with which he was comforted by you, as he told us of your longing, your mourning, your zeal for me, so that I rejoiced still more (2 Cor. 7:5–7).

Just as Paul rejoiced to receive a good report from Timothy about the Thessalonians' endurance, he was comforted in his afflictions when he was finally reunited with Titus. Titus, having

---

13 Even so, Paul had the further hope that he would return one day and supply what was lacking in their faith through ongoing instruction (1 Thess. 3:10).

14 While there are multiple examples of Paul being distracted away from pioneer evangelism for the sake of existing churches, there's a striking lack of complementary examples where Paul intentionally left a struggling church for the sake of pushing into an unreached area. See Paul Bowers, "Fulfilling the Gospel: The Scope of the Pauline Mission," *JETS* 30/2 (June 1987): 190–93.

been encouraged by the Corinthians' positive response to Paul's letter, passed on the good news. They had been grieved by Paul's rebuke. But they had repented of their wrong. They were, once again, reconciled to God and their apostle. The encouragement Titus received from God[15] had been shared with Paul.

This story provides the backdrop, then, for Paul's blessing of the God "who comforts us in all our affliction, so that we may be able to comfort those who are in any affliction, with the comfort with which we ourselves are comforted by God" (2 Cor. 1:4). And Paul's hope for the Corinthians was for them to share in the same experience of grace. He wanted them to no longer avoid shame or shrink back from suffering, but to embrace it. Because if they did, they too would share in God's comfort (2 Cor. 1:7).

Triumphant Wanderings

One of the more memorable mission trips that I've been on took place in the Kurdish region of the Middle East. Our team of six planned to visit a handful of cities, striking up conversations with whomever we met along the way. Our desire was that some of those chance meetings would lead to opportunities to explain the gospel. We carried copies of the Bible, Christian literature, and the *Jesus* film in multiple languages, in case anyone showed interest.

Our original itinerary had us driving northward to some remote towns in a mountainous region, in a place where there were no known Christians or missionaries. However, before our trip even started, an unexpected blizzard closed the mountain pass we needed to cross. Without much of a contingency plan in place, we decided to head in the opposite direction. Our first stop was a small town,

---

15 Initially, this was no doubt a terribly unpleasant mission for Titus.

where we managed to talk with a few shopkeepers about the gospel. Next, we headed southward to a midsized city, hoping for even more opportunities.

As soon as we arrived, our team split into two groups. We prayed as we walked, and we talked with folks as we prayed. But at least for our group, almost everyone we encountered seemed either uninterested or strangely aloof. After a few hours on our feet with almost no positive conversations to show for it, we decided to duck into a grocery store for a snack. After picking up and paying for a Snickers—one of my favorites—I headed out the door.

But then, just as we were exiting the store, three police vehicles pulled up to the curb. Immediately, six officers stepped out with semiautomatic rifles. They asked for IDs. They asked what we were doing. They asked to look in our backpacks—still full of Christian materials. There was no denying what we were up to. They told us to come with them.

What unfolded next is anything but an incredible story of missionary courage or suffering. In fact, my first memory at the police station involves sitting down and searching for my still-unopened Snickers. I thought to myself, *Not going anywhere for a while*, then took a bite.

After a few minutes of waiting, the police brought us into a room for questioning. We were told that Hezbollah had called to complain about us being in town. The terrorist group had threatened to act if the police didn't stop us. That's why they'd picked us up outside the store. And that's why they were going to kick us out of their town. The next morning, an official escort would follow our van until we had left their province entirely.

However, aside from one grumpy and threatening foreign affairs officer who didn't want to waste his Saturday dealing with us, the police in general weren't overly antagonistic. In fact, while walking through the station, one of them pulled me aside and asked if he could have a DVD from my bag. "I've heard about Jesus," he whispered, "and I've always wanted to watch that film."

One of the forgotten and rarely understood sufferings of a missionary is that of constantly being on the move. Our paths are regularly redirected. Our lives are endlessly uprooted. We start out for one city only to end up in another. We feel led to one country only to be supplied a different assignment. We pray about reaching one people group only to be denied residency among them. We learn one language only to need a different dialect. We start a local business only to lose permits. We find the perfect apartment only to have our lease expire. We finally settle into effective ministry only to contract a virus. We plan our ways only to have God direct our steps.

Yes, this is God's doing. The constant change of plans and itineraries isn't necessarily a sign of missionary failure. To be sure, we shouldn't make excuses for lack of research and preparedness. Missionaries too easily play the "flexibility" card to justify inadequate planning and reckless practice. However, what many Westerners struggle to realize is that everyday life in much of the world is still entirely unpredictable. Anything from roadblocks to riots to rabies can overturn a month's worth of preparation in a matter of minutes. Furthermore, when someone is, like Paul, led by the Spirit and encountering Satanic opposition, their travels will almost inevitably look more like wilderness wanderings than the optimized route provided by a navigation app.

The Corinthians couldn't understand this. They were frustrated that Paul reneged on his prior plans to visit them (2 Cor. 1:15–17). This was one more reason why they began to question Paul's reliability. He seemed fickle. If God had been with him and if God's word had been in him, surely his plans would have been immutable. But Paul insisted the opposite. His faithfulness to God, personal integrity, and commitment to them were demonstrated by his willingness to adjust plans and relinquish his preferences. He showed genuine love for them by his flexibility.

In fact, Paul used his example of leaving Troas to defend this reality in his ministry. When he was distracted and his travel diverted, Paul believed that God was in it. "Thanks be to God," he exclaimed, "who in Christ always leads us in triumphal procession, and through us spreads the fragrance of the knowledge of him everywhere" (2 Cor 2:14).

With God there are no wasted journeys.

In her book *Glorious Weakness*, Alia Joy reflects on this truth and the struggle many missionaries face when trying to communicate with individuals and churches back home. As an Asian American missionary kid who grew up on the field, she's seen her parents make difficult decisions and take unwanted detours. Serving with YWAM, their family initially moved from the United States to Holland, then later transferred to Pokhara, Nepal. However, while in Nepal, Alia was diagnosed with acute lymphoblastic leukemia. The family evacuated, taking her to the Netherlands for treatment. Eventually, they relocated back to Hawaii.

Along the way—in addition to the challenges of suffering and illness—their family had to deal with the untold cost of displacement and constant upheaval. But perhaps most difficult of all, they had to reckon with confusion, shame, and frustration as their supporters struggled to comprehend their purpose, their decisions, and their pain. From her perspective, Alia found people back home unable to truly understand, perhaps even unwilling to relate. "We were devastated by those in the church who refused to come near because," she writes, "our pain was too raw. And besides, 'everyone knows you can't take small children to a third world country without something bad happening.'"[16]

In her experience, American evangelicals are much like the Corinthians.[17] They live in a society that despises lack and distrusts the weak, that shames insufficiency and only glories in grief once it's gone.

Confirmed by Suffering, Renewed by Glory

When Paul says that Christ always led him in triumphal procession, he is confronting this perspective head-on. His imagery, rather than engendering confidence, likely shocked and appalled his Corinthian readers. During the Roman period, the triumphal procession was a well-known cultural spectacle that was simultaneously political and religious. Heroes would return from battle to revel in the spoils of war. In it, the victorious general would lead a parade in view of his fellow citizens as his conquered foes, now in chains, trailed behind him in shame. Eventually, the lengthy procession would conclude with the execution of the defeated, a pleasing sacrifice offered in worship and thanksgiving to the gods.[18]

What's so striking about Paul's use of this analogy is that he did not equate himself with the conquering general but with the conquered foe. Christ was the victor, and Paul the spoils. In fact, Paul recognized that Christ's triumph over him—going back to his Damascus road experience—spelled his defeat and ultimate death

---

16 Alia Joy, *Glorious Weakness: Discovering God in All We Lack* (Grand Rapids, MI: Baker, 2019), 69.

17 Western theology tends to ask why God allows suffering more than how he uses it. See Paul Borthwick, *Western Christians in Global Mission: What's the Role of the North American Church?* (Downers Grove, IL: IVP, 2012), 147.

18 For an explanation of the cultural background and theological significance of this triumphal procession, see Scott Hafemann, *2 Corinthians: The NIV Application Commentary* (Grand Rapids, MI: Zondervan, 2000), 106–12.

from the beginning. His life was destined to become a sacrificial offering, not to pagan deities but to God. Through Christ's triumph over Paul, God was spreading the fragrance of the knowledge of Christ wherever he went (2 Cor. 2:14). Paul's suffering became the vehicle for the gospel's advance.

With this vivid imagery, then, we can see how Paul evaluated his own ministry. He wasn't trying to paint a rosy picture for the Corinthians. In a sense, they were right about him. When he was constantly moving from place to place, whenever he changed course and missed a planned stop, or even when he escaped from trouble by scurrying down a wall, it didn't display glory. It smelled of shame. And when Paul was constantly suffering, dealing with physical affliction and emotional anguish, when he was in danger every hour and dying every day (1 Cor. 15:30–31), it didn't project power. It revealed weakness.

But that's the point. Contrary to the Corinthians' opinion, Paul's weakness didn't diminish his effectiveness. The sacrifice of his life was producing a sweet-smelling fragrance of life unto life. It's through his suffering and shame that others were being delivered from death. In other words, the things that should have made Paul lose heart—his suffering, weakness, and shame—were actually the source of his confidence, his ground for boasting, and the means God was using to magnify his power.

This is the core of Paul's defense of his apostolic ministry and missionary agenda. It's "about power in weakness, strength through suffering, about life through death, about triumph through seeming defeat. In short, it is about embodying the message of the cross."[19] What Paul communicates to the Corinthians is that, rather than

---

19 John B. Polhill, *Paul and His Letters* (Nashville: B&H, 1999), 257. As Schreiner puts it, "Suffering was not a side effect of Paul's mission; rather it was at the very center of his apostolic

undermine the gospel, his crucified life is the means for confirming its claims. And not only that, Paul's argument is that his faithful suffering also confirms his own apostolic ministry.[20] In this letter, Paul, who would much rather be commended by God—if not also by the Corinthians—feels compelled to commend himself. But he chooses to do so by pointing to the afflictions he endured (2 Cor. 6:4–5). As Don Howell concludes, "Paul's sufferings *authenticate* him as God's servant, *identify* him with the crucified and risen Christ, and *edify* the church. One who aspires to lead, that is, to impact others for the kingdom of God, must imitate Paul, who himself imitates Christ (1 Cor. 11:1)."[21]

Some years ago I taught the book of Acts to a group of pastors overseas. When we considered the life of Paul, we looked together at the topic of his apostleship. We discussed how, on occasion, he was forced to defend his role and commend his ministry. "How did Paul authenticate his apostleship?" I asked. True, Paul believed his affirmation and authority were from God alone. But his service to Christ was proven and confirmed by his faithful suffering for others. This is what separated Paul from false teachers. False teachers are known not only for seeking approval from others, but also for taking advantage of them. They're known for living in comfort and preferring prosperity. They're known for seeking glory now.

As I shared Paul's self-assessment, the room fell silent. Eyes widened. Eventually, heads began to nod. Churches in that country—

---

evangelism. His distress validated and legitimated his message, demonstrating the truth of the gospel." See Schreiner, *Paul*, 87.

20 "The apostle's legitimacy appears not in the power of his personality, not in his spiritual experience, not in his commissioning by the right ecclesiastical authorities, but only in the extent to which his life and preaching represent the crucified Jesus." See C. K. Barrett, *The Second Epistle to the Corinthians* (London: A & C Black, 1986), 30.

21 Don N. Howell Jr., "Paul's Theology of Suffering," in *Paul's Missionary Methods*, eds. Robert L. Plummer and John Mark Terry (Downers Grove, IL: IVP, 2012), 101.

and in much of the world—are overrun with prosperity preachers who claim the role of apostle but look nothing like one. They preach the cross but refuse to take it up. They claim that signs and wonders demonstrate their anointing, yet they distance themselves from any suffering.[22] They'll identify with Christ in his triumph, but they would never fall in line with his shameful procession. As Jesus would say, they love the glory that comes from people more than the glory that comes from God (John 12:43).

And, as Alia Joy notes, this is a danger for all of us—especially those of us in the West. We need to understand that the path to glory leads through participation in Christ's sufferings:

> When we identify with Christ's suffering, we count the cost. We realize we will be uncomfortable more than we'll be comfortable. We'll be displaced more than we'll be settled. We will be offended, we will be frustrated, we will be misunderstood. Yet still, we are called to rejoice when we share Christ's suffering because we are promised glory revealed.[23]

This is the key. We must set our hope fully on the grace that will be ours at the revelation of Christ (1 Pet. 1:13; 4:13). This is the hope that enables us to endure and not lose heart. How else is it that Paul's outer self could be wasting away, yet his inner self was being renewed day by day? (2 Cor. 4:16). How could he even talk about such inner peace, comfort, and renewal when his self-described afflictions included inner turmoil and his constant anxiety for all

---

22 "Paul maintains that one must suffer for the life of Jesus to be revealed. Signs and wonders are not evil, but in themselves they do not provide a basis for legitimacy since those who are evil can also perform the miraculous (2 Thess 2:9)." See Schreiner, *Paul*, 96.

23 Joy, *Glorious Weakness*, 112.

the churches? It's because Paul believed that "this light momentary affliction is preparing for us an eternal weight of glory beyond all comparison" (2 Cor. 4:17).[24]

The logic here is crucial. Paul was renewed in spirit despite indescribable affliction—a burden beyond description—because it was producing for him a reward with an even greater weight. In the words of David Calhoun, "It is not merely that troubles are followed by glory; our affliction is adding to the coming glory to be ours."[25] This is the correlation of suffering to glory. When we suffer with Christ, we are also honored with him (Rom. 8:17). When we faithfully endure trials, it results in a greater weight of glory that's beyond comprehension.[26]

Paul's theology of suffering sees a direct correlation between the extent of our afflictions and the extent of God's grace. "For *as* we share abundantly in Christ's sufferings, *so* through Christ we share abundantly in comfort too" (2 Cor. 1:5). The more we participate in Christ's afflictions, the more we participate in his comfort. And we experience that comfort *during* our trials—in our inner

---

24 Some commentators understand the Greek conjunction *gar* (translated "for" at the beginning of the verse) as explanatory. Others understand it as grounding or supporting the previous verse. For a thorough argument that faithful suffering leads to greater glory and authority in the kingdom, and that such reward is the basis for Christian endurance, see Josef Tson, *Suffering, Martyrdom, and Rewards in Heaven* (Wheaton, IL: The Romanian Missionary Society, 2000).

25 David B. Calhoun, "The Hope of Heaven," in *Heaven*, eds. Christopher W. Morgan and Robert A. Peterson (Wheaton, IL: Crossway, 2014), 252. As John Piper writes, "There seems to be a connection between the suffering endured and the degree of glory enjoyed." See John Piper, *Let the Nations Be Glad: The Supremacy of God in Missions* (Grand Rapids, MI: Baker, 1993), 89.

26 When speaking earlier about his incredible afflictions in Ephesus, Paul communicated the intense weight of the burden he bore by using the Greek *hyperbole* (2 Cor. 1:8). Here, in 2 Cor. 4:17, he reintroduces the idea of weight, now in reference to glory, but employs *hyperbole* twice, demonstrating that our glory will surpass our suffering. See also the footnote in Barnett, *The Second Epistle to the Corinthians*, 252.

self—as we're assured by the hope of what our faithful endurance will one day produce. On that day, having shared in Christ's glory, we'll look back at all our past sufferings as nothing but a light load. They won't even be worth comparing (Rom. 8:18).

Importing Our Fears and Our Comforts

It would be hard to overstate the importance for missionaries to have a robust theology of suffering and glory. For one, Christ's ambassadors today are increasingly deployed to regions where they must be prepared for persecution. In much of the world, the rise of radical Islamist terrorism and Hindu nationalism present a credible threat to foreign workers. Furthermore, the necessary focus on unreached people groups is pushing missionaries into places that are, not surprisingly, the hardest to reach—usually because they're the most dangerous. When missionaries go to such places, safety and comfort are luxuries they leave behind. Peril isn't potential; it's perpetual.

When we work in those areas, escape and evacuation can't be the obvious or only solution whenever there's a situation of elevated risk. This doesn't mean that fleeing persecution is always wrong. Paul's example was far more nuanced and his approach incredibly situational (including his flight from Damascus). Sometimes the wisest and best course of action is to leave, especially when it involves the health and safety of spouses, children, or local believers. However, we must also recognize that it's impossible to avoid risk entirely. Jesus sends us out as sheep among wolves. Risk is intrinsic to our mission.

However, danger isn't confined just to difficult places. Nor are the threats purely external. Western missionaries themselves—even the best of them—carry the virus of prosperity theology latent within them. And we easily transmit it to others wherever we serve. This can happen simply by our observable lifestyle, as we instinctively gravitate toward comfort and ease in seemingly innocuous decisions about housing and entertainment, education and healthcare. Like it or not, local believers will interpret from us a Christian perspective of suffering and glory whether we overtly teach it or not.

I've known Western missionaries, working in countries with moderate persecution, who were sometimes mystified by the inability of new believers to endure hardship. Expat workers expressed frustration with locals who shied away from suffering or ran away from pain. They also wondered why those who claimed to follow Jesus would prefer to remain secret, never telling their family members or friends about the Savior. But the sad irony I observed was that sometimes—in those very circumstances—the missionaries themselves had modeled the same secretive identity, the same avoidance of suffering, and the same inability to endure. Sadly, their new disciples weren't diverting from the path. They were simply following their lead.

As a result, I've come to consider some of the ways Western missionary colonization still happens. Sure, we're no longer exporting pews and pipe organs. We're beyond that. But we do import our comforts and our fears. We implicitly inculcate others with our timidity, secrecy, contingency, and luxury. The great danger of cultural colonization isn't gone; it's only changed. We're still making disciples in our image.[27]

Anna Hampton, an American who's spent nearly a decade living and working in Afghanistan, sees this as a real problem for the

---

27 It is a fallacy that foreign missionaries can somehow avoid imposing their beliefs, ideas, or patterns of behavior upon nationals. As in parenting, such influence is unavoidable.

West. Her book *Facing Danger: A Guide through Risk* discusses the challenges for cross-cultural workers who leave comfortable, affluent, and "safe" countries to go to difficult regions. She notes how Westerners come from risk-averse and litigious societies with insurance policies and contingencies for everything.[28] But Christian missionaries must be those who demonstrate courage and resilience in times of distress and danger. They must portray the cross, not only by witnessing to the sufferings of Christ, but also by their willingness to suffer with him. According to Scott Sunquist, "Much is communicated about the gospel of salvation through a weak, poor, and suffering servant. Less is communicated about the gospel through a comfortable and wealthy short-term visitor. The call to missionary service is a call to come and die."[29]

The film *A Hidden Life* is a passionate and poetic retelling of a peasant family's life in Austria during World War II. Inspired by the prison letters of Franz Jägerstätter, the movie recounts the true story of his refusal to join the Nazi army and swear allegiance to Hitler. Much of the narrative follows Franz's relationship with his wife, Franziska, as they deliberate together about this excruciating choice. One unmistakable feature of the film, written and directed by Terrence Malick, is the stunning cinematography that juxtaposes light and dark, joy and pain, the vast and gentle flora of a bucolic Alpine countryside with the bleak confines of Franz's cell of torment.

But for me, the most poignant moment in the story came earlier, before Franz entered prison, as he pondered his Christian

---

28 Anna Hampton, *Facing Danger: A Guide through Risk* (New Prague, MN: Zengadi Press, 2016), 8–9.

29 Scott W. Sunquist, *Understanding Christian Mission: Participation in Suffering and Glory* (Grand Rapids, MI: Baker, 2013), 409.

responsibility—and ability—to suffer in ignominy and seeming inconsequence. Wrestling with what he should do, Franz turned to the only place he could think of for wisdom and counsel in such a crisis. He went to the church, first to his priest and then to the bishop.

However, when Franz traveled to speak with the bishop, he found a cowardly man in his own kind of prison. "I think he was afraid," Franz tells his wife upon return to their village. Coerced by Nazi authorities, the bishop had already committed to melting church bells for bullets. He had hoped that such concessions might make the regime more tolerant, that he would forestall any further oppression and distress for himself. But he was fighting a losing battle. Priests were being sent to concentration camps. Church processions were banned. Without a say, having lost all influence, the bishop didn't know what else to do.

Back at home and silently contemplating his conversation, we watch as Franz walks with his cane along a narrow path that traces a steep, emerald hill. Along the trail stands a solitary, wayside shrine. It's an unadorned crucifix carved from wood. Just as Franz is about to pass it by, he stops. Turns back. Looks up. The cross arrests his gaze.

Immediately, Malick shifts the scene—in a carefully choreographed sequence—and we find Franz in a stone sanctuary, ornately embellished with colorful portraits and an elaborate, golden altar. But he is not alone. He's there with a painter. Together with Franz, we listen to the artist's musings:

> I paint all this suffering but I don't suffer myself. I make a living of it. What we do is just create sympathy. We create admirers. We don't create followers.

Christ's life is a demand. You don't want to be reminded of it. So we don't have to see what happens to the truth. A darker time is coming when men will be more clever. They won't fight the truth. They'll just ignore it.

I paint their comfortable Christ with a halo over his head. How can I show what I haven't lived? Someday I might have the courage to venture. Not yet. Someday I'll paint the true Christ.

Way Down

Why is it that missionaries have such a hard time painting the true Christ? Why is it that we're so ill-equipped, so unprepared, to take up our cross and die in the triumphal procession of our Lord's mission? Why do we paint the comfortable Christ?

These are difficult questions. And I hesitate to offer solutions as if they were simple. I also offer my thoughts with a healthy dose of humility, finding myself often in the place of the painter, wondering whether I might have the courage to venture. But many of us may also find ourselves in the place of the bishop. Franz comes asking difficult questions. Sadly, the church doesn't always give good answers. One of the reasons for this, according to Romanian theologian Josef Tson, is that, for a long time, Western evangelicals have only had a partial theology of suffering.[30] We've made heaven a participation trophy and removed any incentive of glory.

But what enables us to endure if not the affirmation, encouragement, and comfort of God (1 Pet. 5:10; Phil. 2:1)? What encourages a farmer to hard work if not the reward of his crops? What inspires an enlisted man if not the pleasure of his commanding officer? What compels the athlete if not the cheers of the crowd and the

---

30 "Unfortunately, the faith in great rewards for sacrifice and self-sacrifice has almost disappeared from modern Christianity." See Tson, *Suffering*, 92.

vision of our Lord at the finish line, waiting to crown us with the prize? This is how Paul encouraged Timothy to share in Christ's sufferings (2 Tim. 2:3–6). Can we do any better?

Our theology of suffering is inadequate if it merely acknowledges that God's servants, like Paul, are called to a life of heartache, humiliation, and affliction. It's insufficient if it simply recognizes that health, wealth, and prosperity are not guaranteed to Christ's ambassadors in this life. What we also need to grasp, along with the Corinthians, is that God's strength flows through our weakness; the gospel is substantiated, and its emissaries are confirmed, through suffering;[31] and we will experience the reward of glory insofar as we share in Christ's shame (1 Pet. 4:13).[32]

Just as Moses was delivered from Pharaoh in a basket, and just as David escaped from Saul through a wall, Paul believed that God's choice servants experience triumph in ways we would never expect. In fact, this truth is portrayed most clearly in the servant who suffered on that old, rugged cross. According to the Christian gospel, victory comes through defeat. Life through death. As Paul had learned firsthand, the cross precedes the crown. Those who are lifted up must first be lowered down.

---

31 "The real triumphs of the gospel have not been won when the church is strong in a worldly sense; they have been won when the church is faithful in the midst of weakness, contempt, and rejection." See Lesslie Newbigin, *The Open Secret: An Introduction to the Theology of Mission* (Grand Rapids, MI: Eerdmans, 1995), 62.

32 Origen urged suffering believers to endure by dwelling upon and considering "the good which will accrue to us" and one day "outweigh what is merited by the toils of combat," because, as he wrote, we do not serve a parsimonious God. See Origen, *Prayer, Exhortation to Martyrdom*, trans. and annotated by John J. O'Meara (New York: Newman, 1954), 142.

3

Sending and Being Sent

Rome

PAUL'S FORMAL REQUEST arrived by courier, carried by the capable hands of a woman whose proven character was known among the churches of Achaia. "I commend to you our sister Phoebe," Paul included, "a servant of the church at Cenchreae" (Rom. 16:1). Cenchreae, a crucial port just ten kilometers east of Corinth, had been a natural landing spot for Paul during his ministry in Corinth. Phoebe, meanwhile, was a woman of some means. She had been a patron to Paul and his fellow workers. As a trusted partner, Paul was able to provide her with a generous recommendation, asking the Romans to extend gracious hospitality.

However, Phoebe's arrival was only the beginning. Paul was planning his own visit and was requesting his own support. He desired for them, the disparate congregations in Rome, to rally around the gospel and join him in taking its message to new lands. Paul's heart was set on Spain.

Though many of the believers in Rome had never seen Paul, some already knew him very well. Most notably, Priscilla and Aquila, hosts of one of the Roman house churches, had worked alongside Paul years earlier in Corinth. In 49, a disturbance among the Jews in Rome led to their expulsion from the city by an imperial edict of Claudius. But in 54, when Nero ascended to power, the law expired. With the border reopened, it paved the way for Aquila and Priscilla to return to Rome along with many others of the Jewish diaspora.[1]

However, a change in official policy didn't necessarily mean that Jews easily integrated into society—or the church. Believers weren't immune to the prevailing cultural prejudice of the day. In some ways, the obstacles were understandable. After five years of having Gentile-only congregations, the influx of immigrant and resettled Jews was bound to disrupt the status quo. As a result, house groups were divided. Some struggled to live at peace with others. Tertiary issues became primary, including who ate what and when, or who observed one holiday instead of another (Rom. 14:1–10).

Paul knew that such divisions hinder effective mission. If the Romans had a hard time with outsiders or immigrants, they might not be eager to support a work to foreign lands.[2] Despite this challenge, Paul wasn't willing to bypass the imperial capital and cut his own path to the Iberian Peninsula. He desired a harvest among believers in Rome as well as the unreached in Spain (Rom. 1:13–15). So he reminded them of his gospel: that all people, regardless of ethnic background, are sinners shamefully separated from God and under his wrath. We've all fallen short of God's glory. But *anyone* who confesses that Jesus is Lord and believes that God raised him from the dead will be saved (Rom. 10:10–13).

---

1 See F. F. Bruce, *The Book of the Acts* (Grand Rapids, MI: Eerdmans, 1988), 347. See also N. T. Wright, *Paul: A Biography* (San Francisco: Harper One, 2018), 320.

2 Jackson W., *Reading Romans with Eastern Eyes: Honor and Shame in Paul's Message and Mission* (Downers Grove, IL: IVP, 2019), 32–35.

However, for Paul, the burning question was how anyone in Spain could call on a Jesus they didn't know. How would they believe unless someone was sent (Rom. 10:14)?

That was where he came in. Whereas Paul was an apostle of Jesus Christ, commissioned by and accountable to God alone, he was also sent out by and answerable to the church. This meant that he constantly pursued the approval and partnership of others—such as the church in Rome—in order to accomplish his mission.

Seeking Approval from Others

On Thursday, June 28, 1810, a young Adoniram Judson stepped forward at the General Association of Massachusetts Proper, the newly established organization of evangelical Congregationalists convening in Bradford. He stood before the assembly to calmly read a statement on behalf of himself and his three friends seated in the front. "The undersigned members of the Divinity College," he began, "respectfully request the attention of their reverend fathers."

Judson then launched into a brief yet well-articulated defense of "attempting a mission to the heathen." The young men were aware of the difficulties, he said. Their motion was the result of more than a passing whim. This band of brothers had carefully examined the information available to them. They'd consulted church leaders and mentors along the way, receiving their approval. Now, they were prepared to take the next step: offering themselves to be sent out on behalf of the churches. They would submit to the opinion and counsel of the Association:

> Whether, with their present views and feelings, they ought to renounce the object of missions, as either visionary or impracticable; if not, whether they ought to direct their attention to the

Eastern or Western world; whether they may expect patronage and support from a missionary society in this country, or must commit themselves to the direction of a European society; and what preparatory measures they ought to take previous to actual engagement.[3]

This group—totaling seven in all—was unquestionably passionate. Yet their approach was decidedly deliberate. They would not move forward without the express consent of their denomination. However, they needed more than mere affirmation. Without a solid commitment of support, their mission would never be realized. Far-off Asia would not be reached.

One of the unavoidable (and some think, unenviable) tasks of a missionary is to seek the approval and support of others. The reality is that missionaries don't simply work for God's approval alone; they depend upon the affirmation of others. Missionaries are tested, proven, and sent out by the church—and often examined when they return. Missionaries aren't independent agents with their own agenda. Their work is meant to be part of an interdependent *co-mission* where others share in the responsibility and the reward.

So it was for Paul. Like Judson and his compatriots, Paul firmly believed in the necessity of preaching (1 Cor. 9:16) and the desperate state of the lost apart from receiving the gospel (Rom. 1:18–23; 10:13–17). He was also convinced in his own mind that the ultimate approval of his ministry came from God alone. Yet Paul well understood that his mission would be severely limited without the fellowship and partnership of other churches and

---

3 Courtney Anders, *To the Golden Shore: The Life of Adoniram Judson* (Valley Forge, VA: Judson Press, 1987), 70.

individuals—without people such as Phoebe. This led him to seek their affirmation and financial contribution.

But that didn't make asking for money easy. In the case of Paul's fundraising plea to the Corinthians for the poor in Jerusalem, he never mentions the word *money*.[4] When he solicits support elsewhere, there appears to be a similar reticence to make an overt request. In the case of his protracted letter to Rome, Paul reserves it for the very end. When writing to the Philippians—a church with whom he'd had an ongoing partnership for many years—Paul is careful to demonstrate that he isn't out for their money (Phil. 4:17). He doesn't want to come across as needy, grumbling, or discontent (Phil. 4:11).

Nevertheless, Paul was eager for the approval of others. He was especially concerned for individuals and churches to not be ashamed of him and pull back their support as he suffered. Thus, when writing to the Philippians, Paul emphasizes that his gospel ministry wasn't hindered by imprisonment. Instead, what happened to him was resulting in the gospel's advance (Phil. 1:12–14). Similarly, when writing Timothy, Paul urges him to not be ashamed of the testimony of the Lord or of himself, Christ's prisoner (2 Tim. 1:8). Accordingly, he sets forward Onesiphorus as an example of someone who remained loyal, recognizing that God's word could not be bound by Paul's chains (2 Tim. 1:16; 2:9).

Essentially, Paul didn't want his many supporters to be like the Corinthians—a church hesitant to associate with a suffering servant. This was a source of deep grief and frustration for the apostle as he composed 2 Corinthians. Having spent much of the letter defending his integrity and ministry to the church he fathered, Paul

---

4 2 Cor. 8–9 seems to be "written in very labored and tortured Greek." See Wright, *Paul*, 308.

concludes, "I have been a fool! You forced me to it, for I ought to have been commended by you" (2 Cor. 12:11). You can almost hear the exasperated tone of the jilted apostle: *How could you have second thoughts about me?*

As the previous chapter considered, the Corinthians questioned Paul's authority and apostleship in part because of his weakness and suffering. They couldn't understand why he wouldn't receive personal funds for his preaching or boast in his strengths. Rather than exalt himself—and them through him—Paul always seemed to lower himself, speaking as if he was the least of all the apostles (1 Cor. 15:9). Within the Corinthian culture, Paul's behavior must have been incomprehensible.

Yet Paul could easily counter with a similar argument toward them. In honor-shame cultures, groups are expected to guard their collective honor by venerating their leader. This was the Corinthians' assumed role. As the fruit of Paul's ministry, they should have been the first to defend his reputation as their apostle. As his spiritual children, they should have recognized and revered their father in the faith.[5] Paul shouldn't have been forced to commend himself. That was their responsibility!

However, as Paul repeatedly made clear, he didn't seek their affirmation for the sake of recognition or even remuneration. Surely they should have been able to see that his refusal to receive their money demonstrated as much (2 Cor. 12:14–18). Paul was ultimately concerned for the Corinthians' well-being, like a parent for a child.[6] True, he wasn't captive to their approval. But he did actively

---

5   See David B. Capes, Rodney Reeves, and E. Randolph Richards, *Rediscovering Paul: An Introduction to His World, Letters and Theology* (Downers Grove, IL: IVP, 2007), 29–33.

6   Strikingly, Paul rarely placed money and ministry in the sphere of a patron-client transaction, preferring instead to emphasize the loving context of familial relations (1 Cor. 4:14–15; 2 Cor. 12:14–15; 1 Thess. 2:6–8).

pursue it.[7] Paul knew that if they rejected him and his gospel, they did so at their own peril. Like a straying and self-confident child, they were flirting with danger if they sought to assert their independence.

Not Many Should Become Missionaries

Years ago, I had a meeting with a national pastor as well as a Canadian missionary at a church building in one of the most unreached countries in the world. Visiting with me were a handful of seminary students who were curious about missions. Our hosts were nearly triple our age, having spent their lives serving Christ in the Middle East and Europe.

After some initial greetings, we sat down on metal folding chairs in their modest fellowship room. The small space was filled by a long, narrow table covered with a plastic tablecloth and steaming cups of tea. As we drank together, the two men answered our questions and offered their perspective on a variety of issues related to overseas ministry. But one of their comments stood out the most. "We don't necessarily want more missionaries," the pastor cautioned. "We want missionaries who come alongside the national church and work with us."

His words might seem counterintuitive. *In one of the most unreached areas of the world, don't we need more workers?* But my national friend wasn't necessarily against all foreign missionaries. What he was saying is that we need the right kind of missionaries. We need those who aren't driven by an independent spirit but who are humble enough to work with others. We need missionaries who

---

7 Quoting Murphy-O'Connor, Garland comments, "'Ministry has two facets, the activity of the apostle and the receptivity of the community.' Paul is concerned about both in this letter." See David E. Garland, *2 Corinthians* (Nashville: B&H, 1999), 28.

listen to wisdom and who respect the wishes of local believers. We need missionaries who desire, and who are willing to wait for, the approval of others—even and especially those outside their culture.[8]

According to Michael Griffiths, writing over a generation ago, the kind of missionary the world needs is

> not just one of those bluff, genial, well-meaning Christian men who is unfortunately unable to speak the language and seems rather clueless, but someone who has served an apprenticeship with the national churches and can communicate effectively, using not only the language, but also the thought patterns of the people.[9]

Wherever I've traveled around the world, I've found national Christians with a similar opinion. They're burnt-out on Western missionaries who parachute in with little or no concern for meaningful partnership and with little planning beyond the first two years. Perhaps not surprisingly, these missionaries often misfire. The results they tout to supporters back home are often skewed or suspect, in part because the missionaries themselves are unaware of hidden cultural dynamics within the host community. Even the genuine fruit they do experience is prone to wither on the vine, precisely because they're disconnected from the life of the national church.

Citing these concerns and others, I've personally heard from national leaders on at least three continents—even in unreached

---

8   See the chapter devoted to this topic in Paul Borthwick, *Western Christians in Global Mission: What's the Role of the North American Church?* (Downers Grove, IL: IVP, 2012), 157–79. However, listening to locals cannot outweigh listening to Scripture.

9   As quoted in David J. Hesselgrave, *Paradigms in Conflict: 10 Key Questions in Christian Missions Today* (Grand Rapids, MI: Kregel, 2005), 207.

areas—who all say essentially the same thing: "Please don't send more missionaries."[10] By that they don't mean, "Never come." They mean, ask before you come. Be a learner before you arrive. Listen to local advice. Partner with a national congregation. The paternalism of past generations won't be resolved simply by doing our own thing or working in isolation with one national, then calling it a partnership. Missionaries should pursue genuine relationship, fellowship, and ongoing collaboration with local churches and their leaders.

But, as we know, local partnerships aren't always possible. Missionaries, like Paul, are those especially burdened to go to places where there are no churches or no known believers. Even in those situations, however, there's a significant opportunity for us to follow Paul's example when, desiring to go to Spain, he sought the help and support of a culturally and geographically nearer congregation. In almost every situation, missionaries today can find a similar near-culture church, much like the one in Rome, with whom they could partner to reach the unreached.[11]

However, that's not enough. We also need to take seriously the suggestions of our brothers and sisters around the world and consider sending fewer workers. In recent decades, the ease of modern travel, the relative wealth of Western Christians, and a genuine desire to serve have all combined to unleash a generation of untrained and unproven witnesses to the world. This unprecedented rise of cross-cultural Christian workers is what Ralph Winter termed the "amateurization" of missions.[12] We're living at a time in church

---

10 Interestingly, I remember hearing the opposite only once. In a remote area of a "reached" country a local pastor inquired, "Why don't you send missionaries anymore? We need your help!"

11 From Paul's pattern, it's a safe assumption that he expected to take a Roman believer along with him to Spain, perhaps to help with Latin.

12 For a discussion of this topic, see Hesselgrave, *Paradigms*, 203–38.

history where anyone and everyone can be sent on short-term ministry trips. We also have an abundance of midterm and long-term missionaries with little theological or missiological training.

Recently I was in a large missions festival in Vancouver, British Columbia. A young couple introduced themselves. They excitedly shared how they were making plans to move to Zambia. They wanted to open an orphanage, provide business training and opportunities for women, start a church and perhaps a school. They were wide-eyed and ready. But the more we talked, the more it became clear that they had little or no contact with the local church or other missionaries in Zambia. They had almost no training, no model to follow. The plan was basically to show up and get started—but they needed help!

This story repeats itself in personal conversations time and again. A newly married couple raising money to fight sex-trafficking in Thailand. A medical doctor training pastors in India. A recent graduate from business school catalyzing a church planting movement in Europe. An English-speaking youth group mentoring other youth at a camp in Central America. A local church adopting a people group in remote Central Asia. And many of them have limited theological or cultural equipping for their work.

Simply having a heart to help and a plane ticket in hand doesn't make one a missionary. Sharing the gospel or being passionate about reaching the unreached, while admirable, is not what qualifies someone to be sent out. As Andy Johnson argues, "Only some have a moral claim on the local church's financial support."[13] Only some are missionaries.[14] In the same way that we're not all called to

---

13 Andy Johnson, *Missions: How the Local Church Goes Global* (Wheaton, IL: Crossway, 2017), 39.

14 The term "missionary" is derived from the Latin *missio*, which conveys the act of sending. In Greek, the equivalent term is *apostolos*, or apostle, "a messenger who is sent." To be a missionary or apostle is a unique office or role based on Christ's gifts to the church (Eph.

be a church's paid pastor, not everyone is called to be a supported worker.

There are many practical reasons for this, but most significant is that, in God's kingdom, leaders must give an account for their labors. The care of souls increases one's obligation before God (Heb. 13:17). Teachers will face a stricter judgment (James 3:1). But if it's true, as James reasons, that not many should become teachers, surely it also means that not many should become missionaries.

Test, Affirm, and Send

When Paul acknowledged to the Corinthians his inadequacy as a minister of the gospel (2 Cor. 2:16), he wasn't making an argument for incompetent missionaries. But sometimes Western Christians speak as if what qualifies someone for ministry is the recognition that they aren't really qualified. We've equated the admission of inability with the virtue of humility. Similarly, I've seen churches eagerly encourage all who feel called to missions yet hesitate to place any requirements of education or experience upon them. We easily affirm their willingness to sacrifice without considering their ability to serve. Even more concerning, some Christians exult in their neediness and brokenness as if those attributes are what make them most useful in the kingdom.

But while Paul boasted in weakness, recognizing his insufficiency for the missionary task and his utter dependence on the Spirit (2 Cor. 3:4–6), he could also boast in the quality of his efforts, his

---

4:11–16). In the New Testament, the designation of apostle is not limited to the twelve but includes others sent out as representatives of churches (Acts 14:14; Rom. 16:7; 2 Cor. 8:23; Gal. 1:19; Phil. 2:25; 1 Thess. 2:6). The early church also used the term *apostolos* for itinerant evangelists (Didache 11.3–6). For a fuller discussion of this topic, see Daniel Sinclair, *A Vision of the Possible* (Colorado Springs: Authentic, 2006), 251–59, and George W. Peters, *A Biblical Theology of Missions* (Chicago: Moody, 1972), 246–58.

diligent hard work, and the results that were produced through God's Spirit in him (1 Cor. 15:10). Paul didn't assume that human inability or inefficiency automatically led to God's blessing. Most importantly, he didn't equate repeated struggles and moral failure with physical inadequacy or weakness. Paul could talk about God using weak jars of clay (2 Cor. 4:7). But in order to be useful, those same vessels needed to be honorable, holy, and fit for the Master's use (2 Tim. 2:21). This is the pattern we see repeated throughout Scripture. God has high expectations for the shepherds of his people and the stewards of his word. To whom much is given, much will be required (Luke 12:48).

Therefore, those whom we send should be competent in the Scriptures and of good character.[15] And when it comes to identifying and sending the right kind of people, the onus is on the local church. They must do the work of affirming missionaries who qualify.[16]

A good example of this is Paul and Barnabas. When the gospel initially spread through Jews scattered by persecution, Barnabas was sent by the church in Jerusalem to Antioch to observe what was happening. He was undoubtedly chosen for his character, as someone filled with the Spirit and knowledgeable in the Scriptures (Acts 11:24).[17] But as Barnabas observed Gentiles coming to faith,

---

15 "Heresy, confusion, and syncretism most often occur at the edge of gospel expansion. Therefore, that is where we need our best-equipped people." See Johnson, *Missions*, 45.

16 According to Michael Griffiths, "The most that an individual can do is express his *willingness*. Others must determine his *worthiness*. The individual may be *free* to go, but only his church knows if he is really *fitted* to go." As quoted in Hesselgrave, *Paradigms*, 230. I have a related concern when missionary support is derived solely (or almost entirely) from individuals instead of churches.

17 Barnabas may also have been selected because he was a Cypriot Jew (Acts 4:36), as were those who originally traveled to Antioch and preached among the Hellenists there (Acts 11:20).

he felt the need to find Paul in Tarsus. Having already spent almost ten years serving in Syria and Cilicia, Paul and his faithful ministry and calling to the Gentiles were known to Barnabas.[18] Together, they returned to Antioch, where they taught the growing group of believers for a full year.

It's in this context that the Spirit led the church to set apart these two men to be sent out (Acts 13:1–2). Paul wasn't commissioned by the church officially until he had spent fourteen years proving himself through evangelism, teaching, and faithful ministry (Gal. 2:1).[19] If we consider also his lifetime of training in the Hebrew Scriptures even before his Damascus road experience, then our calculation of Paul's ministry preparedness increases significantly. Paul was anything but an amateur. For the church in Antioch, sending Paul meant the sacrifice of sending their best.

But today, churches will send almost anyone. David Hesselgrave sees this as a direct result of missionary "volunteerism"—of widespread and urgent calls for workers to go into the harvest. These impassioned pleas are often punctuated with stories of great need and reinforced by the idea that we're all called to be missionaries. But this represents a confusion of categories. We're not all called to be missionaries. In fact, such a general call to arms is a relatively recent phenomenon and conspicuously absent from the pages of Scripture. According to Hesselgrave, "All New Testament missionaries were personally conscripted by Christ, his apostles and their representatives, or by Holy Spirit-directed churches."[20]

---

18 Acts 9:26–30; 11:25–26; Gal. 1:21.

19 For a reasonably reconstructed timeline of Paul's chronology, see Capes, Reeves, and Richards, *Rediscovering Paul*, 98–101. If you date Paul and Barnabas's visit to Jerusalem in Gal. 2:1–10 and before Acts 13:1, then Paul's ministry was also affirmed by "the pillars" in Jerusalem before he was officially sent out by Antioch.

20 Hesselgrave, *Paradigms*, 215.

This is essential. Local churches must regain their responsibility to prove, affirm, and send qualified missionaries.[21] In the Bible, churches are the ones called upon to have the knowledge and discernment necessary to assess missionaries and their ministries. Churches must test and approve what is good (Phil. 1:9–10; 1 Thess. 5:21). Paul's pattern was to employ workers in ministry who had already been examined and demonstrated themselves as faithful (1 Cor. 16:3; 2 Cor. 8:22; 1 Tim. 3:10; 2 Tim. 2:2). This assumes that some will not pass the test. Some teachers and some ministries are not good and should not be approved. Some are not even from God (1 John 4:1). In such cases, churches are instructed to neither receive them nor support their work (2 John 10).

Here again, the judgment of God on the last day is in view. The Lord will examine ministers for their work (1 Cor. 3:13) and churches for those they commission (1 Tim. 5:22; 2 John 11).[22] This, then, is the connection between Paul seeking ultimate approval from God while also seeking approval from the Corinthians. He wanted them to rightly evaluate the teachers who had infiltrated their congregation. Since Paul deemed them to be false apostles—false missionaries—he intentionally tried to undermine their credibility and mission (2 Cor. 11:12–15). Conversely, Paul hoped that the Corinthians would test his work and find him worthy of their affirmation and support (2 Cor. 13:6).

This responsibility to test supported workers isn't a license to be judgmental. Nor should procuring a church's financial provision be a grueling process, with missionaries regularly running the

---

21 Here I'm borrowing language from Brian Croft, *Test, Train, Affirm & Send into Ministry: Recovering the Local Church's Responsibility in the External Call* (Leominster, UK: Day One, 2010).

22 See D. A. Carson, *A Model of Christian Maturity: An Exposition of 2 Corinthians 10–13* (Grand Rapids, MI: Baker, 2019), 45.

gauntlet to be vetted and maintained. Christians should gladly and generously supply the needs of fellow workers for the faith (3 John 5–8). However, churches must be careful how, and in whom, they invest. They should seek to approve and send those whom God will ultimately approve.[23] Churches are called to test missionaries because God will one day test each of us. We will all give an account for our stewardship. Thus, when Paul was busy defending himself and commending his ministry to the Corinthians, he reminded them that he did so in view of God's judgment and commendation (2 Cor. 12:19).

Sacrificing Vision for the Sake of Commendation

Any discussion of missions and Paul's desire for commendation on the last day must take stock of 2 Corinthians 10:13–18. One would be hard pressed to find another single pericope with more profound insights into Paul's mindset or relevant implications for contemporary missiology. In this passage, having just noted the preference of false teachers to compare themselves with one another and commend themselves by human standards, Paul describes his hope for the Corinthians:

> But we will not boast beyond limits, but will boast only with regard to the area of influence God has assigned to us, to reach even to you. For we are not overextending ourselves, as though we did not reach you. For we were the first to come all the way to you with the gospel of Christ. We do not boast beyond limit in the labors of others. But our hope is that as your faith increases,

---

23 "Paul envisions the community of faith as the earthly counterpart to the divine court of opinion." See Te-Li Lau, *Defending Shame: Its Formative Power in Paul's Letters* (Grand Rapids, MI: Baker, 2020), 152.

our area of influence among you may be greatly enlarged, so that we may preach the gospel in lands beyond you, without boasting of work already done in another's area of influence. "Let the one who boasts, boast in the Lord." For it is not the one who commends himself who is approved, but the one whom the Lord commends. (2 Cor. 10:13–18)

Paul understands that a worker's approval depends on divine commendation and not human opinion. Boasting in one's personal ministry accomplishments doesn't necessarily translate to God's acclaim. This also applies to a local church's evaluation of the apostle (1 Cor. 4:2–5). The Corinthians could turn their back on Paul, but they don't have the final say. The judgment seat of Christ relativizes the views of others—even of ourselves—and frees us to work for an audience of one.[24] When our primary aim is pleasing God, missionaries are released from the burden of pleasing others and producing results for them.

But that doesn't mean Paul wasn't concerned with results. He absolutely was. His ability to boast was connected to (and limited by) his confidence in the fruit of his labors within his field of ministry. Paul would have no reason to boast if he didn't anticipate that God would one day affirm him for his work. Therefore, Paul didn't take a "hands-off" approach to the Corinthian believers once they were reached. Instead, he actively pursued the increase of their faith through an increase of his influence among them.[25] If their

---

24 Paul put little weight in what others thought. "It is a very small thing," he told the Corinthians, "that I should be judged by you or by any human court" (1 Cor. 4:3). However, Paul wasn't flippant toward ecclesial authorities or careless in the way he carried out his ministry (1 Cor. 10:32–33; 2 Cor. 8:20–21).

25 The Greek construction of this verse (15) makes it notoriously difficult to translate. Paul could be saying that he desired (1) that the Corinthians venerate him more (as in the KJV

faith grew, Paul knew it would also expand his joy and boast in the Corinthians on the last day (2 Cor. 1:12–14; cf. 2 Thess. 1:3–4). This is the reason for sending multiple letters, multiple representatives, and even making multiple personal visits (2 Cor. 1:15). By implication, this Pauline approach calls into question church planting strategies wherein missionaries seek to intentionally limit their influence upon local believers. In the case of Corinth, it's helpful to remember that Paul was dealing with well-established congregations that were already reproducing throughout Achaia (such as Cenchreae). By the standards of some missiologists, in such a case Paul should have reduced his influence rather than increase it![26]

However, Paul's stated purpose in his approach is instructive. He desired a greater influence among the Corinthians so that he could take the gospel beyond them.[27] In other words, Paul's missionary vision and ambition to reach the unreached was dependent upon and delayed by the Corinthians' need to increase in faith and discern which apostle to follow. The logic of this paragraph is unmistakable. Paul's inner drive to expand the gospel's borders was restricted by his concern for the Corinthians. They had embraced his gospel and were growing. But they needed to be grounded in

---

and NASB), (2) that his ministry would exert more influence among them (as in the NIV and ESV), or (3) that through them his ministry would expand to new locations. I understand the first and second to be related and more likely since the third would be redundant considering the purpose stated in verse 16.

26 An early example of this would be Roland Allen, *Missionary Methods: St. Paul's or Ours?* (Grand Rapids, MI: Eerdmans, 1962), 149. It should be noted that Allen's advocacy for reducing a missionary's influence over national believers was a reaction to the mission stations and compounds common in his era. It could be argued that his ideas have been overextended by current practitioners.

27 Paul Barnett, *The Second Epistle to the Corinthians* (Grand Rapids, MI: Eerdmans, 1997), 490–91.

the truth in order to fend off false teachers. Only then would Paul feel free to push into new lands.

This reality has significant implications for what it meant for Paul to have God's approval guide his missionary ambition. Paul's ability to boast on the last day was directly tied to his work, to the field God assigned to him. And his confidence in God's commendation was connected to the Corinthians' growth and stability in the faith. Any hope he had of ministry expansion beyond Corinth was conditioned by a prior need for greater ministry influence within Corinth.[28] He prioritized their faith over new fields.[29]

Thankfully, Paul didn't have to sacrifice his pioneering spirit and missionary ambition entirely. His persistent efforts among the Corinthians paid off. With each successive visit and letter, Paul's influence among them did grow, as did their faith. His third trip to Corinth was a success. It lasted a few short months (Acts 20:3), long enough to shore up any nagging concerns and collect his offering for Jerusalem. But only then, having been assured of the Corinthians' stability in the gospel, was Paul released to press into the West. "Opportunity and need had come together. It was time to write another letter."[30]

Paul's epistle to the Romans, his magisterial missionary support letter, was composed during that third visit to Corinth. The chronology here is significant. Paul was only ready to pursue a mission to Spain once he was confident that he had fulfilled his ministry in Corinth (Rom. 15:19–20). That "fulfillment" included far more

---

28 Paul Bowers, "Fulfilling the Gospel: The Scope of the Pauline Mission," *JETS* 30/2 (June 1987):192.

29 "Paul is willing to mortgage his own vision of the future to the needs of the Corinthian church. If God called him to establish a church in Corinth, he cannot abandon that responsibility just because he detects new opportunities and still greater need elsewhere." Carson, *Model*, 101.

30 Capes, Reeves, and Richards, *Rediscovering Paul*, 168–69.

than reaching them, seeing their numbers grow, and even observing the multiplication of churches throughout Achaia. It meant their long-term viability and gospel fidelity. Furthermore—and perhaps equally surprising—Paul was not prepared to go to Spain without first corresponding and cooperating with the Romans.[31] So he sent Phoebe to secure their partnership.

Depending on the National Church

I once had the opportunity to teach for a week at a Bible school in Novi Sad, Serbia. After spending time with a missionary family there, I was reminded of the inevitable challenges that come when you hitch your ministry vision to the national church. In various conversations, they shared about delayed plans, strategic compromises, and even relational struggles. Their decision came at deep personal cost, and they weren't sure, in the end, if it was worth it.

But as we sat around the dinner table on my final night in the country, I tried to encourage them. I thanked them for their evident faith and patience. From my perspective, they were doing missions the right way. They had sacrificed short-term gains, but I could see how it was resulting in long-term effectiveness. By collaborating with the local church, they were building toward unity and doing so in humility. While I'm sure they didn't do so perfectly, they modeled what it looks like to value a genuine partnership that depends on the locals.

Nik Ripken is a missionary and researcher who's spent much of his life working among and learning from persecuted Christians. In the 1980s, he began his ministry in South Africa and Malawi, later moving northward to work with the Somali population of

---

31 It's of interest that Paul, who wrote that he didn't want to build on another's foundation, was instructing the Romans and seeking fruit among them—a church he didn't establish.

SENDING AND BEING SENT

East Africa. Then, in 1998, Ripken started a journey that would take him around the world, interviewing persecuted believers and documenting their experiences of suffering with Christ.[32]

Ripken recounts a story when, after visiting over forty-five countries, he returned to a Muslim context to conduct interviews. He had lined up more than a week of meetings with multiple followers of Jesus. The interviewees were diverse. He visited rural and suburban areas, speaking with old and young, women and men. As he spoke with those believers about their persecution, Ripken also asked a simple question: "What makes a good missionary?" To his surprise, wherever he went, the answer was always the same: "I don't know what makes a good missionary, but I can tell you the name of the man we love."

After ten days of hearing this repeated response from people in five different locations throughout the country, Ripken was desperate for more details. In his final interview, sitting at a table with a group of men, Ripken repeated the same question and received the same answer. But this time he pressed for specifics. He wanted to know what made this missionary so beloved. Eventually, one of the men looked at Ripken and leaned into a firm answer, "You want to know why we love him? We love him because he borrows money from us!" Ripken was stunned silent. The man continued:

When this missionary's father died, he came to us and asked for our help. We didn't have much, but we gathered an offering of love. We bought him a plane ticket so that he could go home to America and bury his father. This man and his family give everything they have to the poor. They struggle to pay rent and

---

32 See Nik Ripken, *The Insanity of God: A True Story of Faith Resurrected* (Nashville: Broadman & Holman, 2012).

school fees, and put meat on the table. And when he has a great need, what does he do? He doesn't go to the other Westerners for money. He comes to us. He comes to the scattered and the poor, he comes to local believers, and he asks for, and gets, our help.[33]

Ripken says that man's testimony made him want to go back to Africa and start all over as a missionary. To be honest, it had a similar effect on me. If I could go back to my missionary years in Central Asia, I'd do some things differently. When making plans about moving to an unreached area, I'd spend more time listening to national churches in the region. When trying to go to a frontier field, I'd request—and wait for—a meaningful local partnership. I wouldn't necessarily surrender my urgency. But I'd want to supplement it with patience and humility. Perhaps most important of all, I'd look for ways to depend on the prayers and support of local Christians. Because, as Ripken learned, it's not enough to listen to national believers. You need to need them.[34]

However, that's not typically how we in the West conceive of sending and being sent. We're very concerned about not creating dependency among the locals whom we serve. The paternalism of the past has made us skittish about doing anything for them. But that doesn't mean we've eliminated dependency in missions. We still supply missionaries with everything they need—which is a wonderful gift—in a system that assumes the missionary's constant reliance on those back home. Consequently, Western workers rarely factor in the possibility of receiving support along the way.[35]

33 Nik Ripken, "What's Wrong with Western Missionaries?," Desiring God (website), September 12, 2016, https://www.desiringgod.org/.

34 See also Borthwick, Western Christians, 132–33.

35 Receiving support along the way is the overwhelming pattern within the New Testament (Rom. 15:24; 1 Cor. 16:6, 11; 2 Cor. 1:16; Titus 3:13; 3 John 5–8). However, this is different than

In the case of the Corinthians, we would be amiss if we assumed that Paul's preference was to never receive support from them.[36] Clearly, he did from Phoebe (Rom. 16:2). Also, on his second visit to Corinth, Paul's original plan was for them to provide for his travel to the next stop (1 Cor. 16:5–6; cf. 2 Cor. 1:16). But, as we've seen, Paul's plans changed. His confidence in the Corinthians wavered. Nevertheless, he still requested their prayer support (2 Cor. 1:11) and still enlisted their participation in the Jerusalem collection (2 Cor. 8–9). He wanted the Corinthians to see themselves as working together with him in his mission beyond Corinth just as he was working together with them to stand firm in their faith (2 Cor. 1:24).

As I consider Paul's ministry model, I don't observe him releasing those in his influence as soon as possible—especially those who were struggling. And I don't come to the conclusion that the ultimate goal of missions is self-sustaining, self-supporting, and self-propagating churches who need nothing from the missionary or sending church. Neither is it the goal to have self-funded missionaries or independent operatives who don't rely on the locals.[37] That's because missions is always a cooperative partnership. Which means the solution to dependency isn't independence. It's *interdependence*.

The Motivation for Our Interdependent Co-Mission

Why did Paul take such a collaborative approach? Was he just naturally a team player? Did he understand collective efforts to

---

Jesus's command for his disciples to *exclusively* receive provision on their journey (Luke 9:1–3; 10:4–7). Those instructions were for a unique historical situation (announcing the kingdom to fellow Jews) and are no longer applicable when the mission becomes global (Luke 22:35–37).

36 "Although Paul did not receive support from a congregation while he was working among them, he did allow them to equip him for his travel to the next mission point." See David E. Garland, *1 Corinthians* (Grand Rapids, MI: Baker, 2003), 757.

37 Furthermore, it makes sense that sending churches would have something to receive or something to learn from newly formed congregations on the field (Rom. 15:27).

be more strategic, effective, or culturally sensitive? Perhaps. But I want to conclude this chapter with one rarely considered reason why Paul enlisted the support of churches to join him through prayer and financial support. He wanted to maximize their reward.

When Paul requests prayer from the Corinthians, he includes this motivation: "You also must help us by prayer, *so that many will give thanks* on our behalf *for the blessing* ["grace" in Greek] granted us through the prayers of many" (2 Cor 1:11). When defending his suffering, he says much the same: "For it is all for your sake, so that *as grace extends* to more and more people *it may increase thanksgiving*, to the glory of God" (2 Cor. 4:15). And when encouraging sacrificial giving to the brothers and sisters in Jerusalem—what he repeatedly called an *act of grace* (2 Cor. 8:6–7, 9)—Paul encourages them with a similar incentive: "[This] will *produce thanksgiving to God . . .* overflowing *in many thanksgivings to God . . .* they will glorify God because of your submission . . . while they long for you and pray for you, *because of the surpassing grace of God* upon you" (2 Cor. 9:11–14).

Paul believed that the Corinthians should graciously partner together with him in his ministry because it would result in grace extending to more and more people. And as that grace extended to others, the Corinthians would share in the benefits (2 Cor. 8:10). Specifically, the people blessed through Paul's ministry would render thanks to God for his grace at work in the Corinthians.

This idea of thanksgiving overlaps with Paul's vision of boasting. As we already explored, Paul expected that on the day of the Lord the Corinthians would boast of him just as he would of them (2 Cor. 1:14). That mutual boasting involves, I believe, giving joyful thanks to God for his grace at work in others. If so, this is precisely what Paul does in nearly all of his letters, wherein he boasts before the Lord by giving thanks to God for believers and churches (1 Cor. 1:4; Phil. 1:3; 1 Thess. 1:2). This connection between thanksgiving and boasting is perhaps most clear in Paul's second epistle to the Thessalonians, where he writes, "We ought always to give thanks to God for you, brothers, as is right, because your faith is growing abundantly. . . . *Therefore we ourselves boast about you* in the churches of God" (2 Thess. 1:3–4).

Many commentators focus only on the vertical dimension of this thanksgiving. It gives glory to God. However, we shouldn't overlook the deep and meaningful horizontal dimension to this act of thanksgiving. Paul gives thanks to God by boasting about the Thessalonians *to others*. To brag about someone in the presence of others is to honor and encourage them. And Paul uses this boast both to praise believers for their faith and to inspire others to imitate their behavior (2 Cor. 7:14; 8:1). Ultimately, Paul's thanksgiving and boast is a foretaste of what he envisions of the last day, when all our work is made manifest (1 Cor. 3:13).[38] He looks forward to the opportunity to stand before Christ, expecting to be proud of his labors (Phil. 2:16), to rejoice in the fruit of his work (1 Thess. 2:19), and for others to give thanks for him to the glory of God.

But that's not all. Paul wants individuals and churches—such as in Corinth, Philippi, and Thessalonica—to share in that joy and glory as well.[39] So he encourages them to pray and sacrifice so that others would thank God for them. He invites them to work

---

38 Te-Li Lau understands that Paul employed shameful rhetoric to allude to God's shaming judgment. Similarly, I think Paul praised believers to foreshadow their future praise before God. See Lau, *Defending Shame*, 116–17.

39 Constantine Campbell sees glory for the Gentiles (and Jews) as a significant endpoint, or *telos*, for Paul's ministry. "As such, Paul is ultimately a servant not only of the church but of glory itself." See Constantine R. Campbell, *Paul and the Hope of Glory: An Exegetical and Theological Study* (Grand Rapids, MI: Zondervan, 2020), 277–78.

together with him, knowing that God will bring their partnership to a completion at the day of Christ (Phil. 1:6).[40] And he asks them to generously give—not because he desires their money, but so they'll share in a harvest and increase their reward (Phil. 4:17; Matt. 10:41).

What makes a good missionary? It isn't just bringing the gospel to new people. It's working together with them for the increase of their faith. And it's inviting them to partner with you as grace extends to the nations—to maximize their joy and crown, all to the praise of God's glorious grace.

---

40 Paul's confidence toward the Philippians expressed in Phil. 1:6 wasn't solely about their individual salvation but included the eternal significance of their partnership in his mission. See G. Walter Hansen, *The Letter to the Philippians* (Grand Rapids, MI: Eerdmans, 2009), 49–51.

4

Seeing the Invisible

Cilicia

A MERE MAN, A MAKER OF TENTS, had seen the eternal dwellings. He had caught a glimpse, if ever so short, of what will be when we trade our earthly shelter—our mortal flesh—for a resurrected abode. But more than an ecstatic vision, this was an actual transport to paradise, a traveling to the highest heaven (2 Cor. 12:1–4). Mortal man had visited a house not made with hands and heard things too wonderful for words, glories beyond expression.

When Saul descended to earth, it wasn't the first time he had returned home after a life-transforming vision. As a young Hebrew, Saul left Tarsus to study in Jerusalem. He had learned at the feet of Gamaliel. He had become an expert in the law of Moses. Among Pharisees, he was the most pharisaical. Among zealous, the most radical. Saul was the kind of son who'd make a mother proud. Educated. Accomplished. Excelling. In his own words, he had reason for confidence "in the flesh" (Phil. 3:4–6). But then everything changed. His encounter with the risen Christ on the way to Damascus dramatically altered his life.

After travels to Arabia and a harrowing escape from Damascus, Saul made a short stop in Jerusalem, then came home to his native Tarsus of Cilicia (Gal. 1:18–21). Cilicia, the Roman province cornering the northeastern Mediterranean coast, was the region where he would spend the next ten years of his life. But when Saul returned, much like a young soldier back from battle, he saw the world differently. Because he saw Messiah differently.

Returning home is difficult for those who come back different. No doubt, it was the same for Saul. Was he a sudden stranger in his old stomping grounds? Was his commitment to evangelism a threat to his tentmaking profession? Did his parents question him? Did extended family, and the broader Jewish community, disown him?

We can't know for sure. But it was then, while Saul was in Cilicia, coming face-to-face with the challenge of following Jesus in his former home, that he was taken away to paradise. When the potential for shame was great, God revealed glories beyond compare. If being knocked down on the Damascus road accounts for Saul's revolutionary redirection in life, then surely this upward call accounts for the apostle's lifelong ability to endure inexpressible suffering and labor with indefatigable zeal.[1] Seeing glory would forever change him.

So, once again, Saul returned home a different man. But to prevent him from being arrogant or self-assured, a thorn in the flesh was given to him (2 Cor. 12:7). It would be his constant companion for the rest of his days, a pricking reminder to trust God's grace in the slump of his weakness. God's strength alone is what would make him sufficient for his mission. Missionaries, of all people, must put no confidence in the flesh but instead look

---

1   See Philip Hughes, *Paul's Second Epistle to the Corinthians* (Grand Rapids, MI: Eerdmans, 1962), 439.

to the power and glory of the unseen. Missionaries are those who rely on God's Spirit.

Affirmed by the Spirit

In 1886, Annie Fraser gave birth to her third son, a boy she named after his father, James. As the daughter of a London businessman, Annie had grown up in a cultured and relatively well-to-do family. At twenty-three, she married an already accomplished veterinary surgeon. Over the years, as their family grew, they decided to leave London and relocate to nearby St. Albans. There, in the breakfast room of their large home, Annie spent untold hours teaching their young children lessons in music, art, and the life of Christ, all the while doing so with a hidden aim. She was praying that one of them would one day become a missionary.

Years later, God answered that prayer. While an engineering student at Imperial College London, James O. Fraser gave his life to Christ and, at the same moment, committed to becoming a missionary. He had grown up under his mother's tutelage and godly example. But it took a small book on missions to profoundly change his view of the world—and of his Lord. Writing of the instant effect that vision had on her son, Annie recalled how James came downstairs from prayer with "his face shining." The Holy Spirit, she observed, had filled his heart with joy. Annie remembered how he quickly grew in faith and became for her a spiritual mentor:

> After Jim's conversion, we had such deep spiritual fellowship. He was a great help to me. We shared spiritual experiences. Indeed, he became my teacher. My progress had been gradual through the years; he seemed a mature Christian right away.

He had so completely given himself to the Lord that he could be filled with the Spirit. He emptied himself—and so the Lord could fill him.[2]

Thus filled with the Spirit, Fraser went on to become one of the most successful missionaries of the twentieth century. Serving with China Inland Mission among the Lisu people, he witnessed a movement of God such that many came to Christ in his lifetime. Even after he succumbed to cerebral malaria in 1938, the church among the Lisu continued to grow, as it does to this day.

If we could ask the apostle Paul what contributed most to his success in mission, surely he would speak of the Holy Spirit. The presence of the Spirit, as God's down payment for future glory, was Paul's source of comfort and hope throughout his constant suffering. Moreover, the basis of Paul's boast—and of his expectation for others to boast in him on the last day—is that God's Spirit was in him. Just as the Spirit's descent on Jesus at his baptism, along with the Father's verbal approval, both affirmed and equipped the Son for ministry, Paul felt that God's affirming word had already been pronounced over him with the dispensing of the Spirit on his life.[3] Thus, when it came to defending his reputation to the Corinthians, Paul asserted: "And it is God who establishes us with you in Christ, and has anointed us, and who has also put his seal on us and given us his Spirit in our hearts as a guarantee" (2 Cor. 1:21–22).

Whereas his opponents wanted to boast about superficial strength and "outward appearance," Paul preferred to boast about what's "in

---

2   As quoted by Geraldine Taylor, *Behind the Ranges: The Story of J. O. Fraser* (Littleton, CO: OMF International, 2012), 25.

3   "Jesus and Paul were encouraged to pursue the costly way of obedience as a result of God's affirmation." See Ajith Fernando, *Jesus Driven Ministry* (Wheaton, IL: Crossway, 2002), 55.

the heart" (2 Cor. 5:12). That is, he would boast only in God's Spirit at work in him. In fact, when forced to commend his ministry to the Corinthians, Paul didn't merely list his Christlike afflictions, hardships, calamities, and weaknesses. He also commended himself through the characteristics of the inner person: "by purity, knowledge, patience, kindness, *the Holy Spirit*, genuine love; by truthful speech, and the power of God; with the weapons of righteousness for the right hand and for the left" (2 Cor. 6:6–7). If Paul needed to prove himself, he would do so by the unmistakable fingerprints of God's Spirit upon his transformed life.

But that's not all. The transformed lives of believers in Corinth also confirmed Paul's ministry. They were the verifiable product of his gospel witness, the reputable references that would vouch for his apostolic resume (1 Cor. 9:2; 2 Cor. 3:1–2). Paul's ministry was authenticated and affirmed by the Corinthians themselves. They were his letter of recommendation, written on human hearts *by the Holy Spirit* (2 Cor. 3:3). Apart from the Spirit's sealing and sanctifying work in them, Paul knew that his efforts would amount to nothing; they would be in vain. Paul, like all of us, was completely inadequate for gospel ministry were it not for the Spirit (2 Cor. 2:16; 3:4–6).

Consequently, the abiding presence of the Spirit supplied Paul with profound confidence and assurance. In a sense, having been set apart by the Spirit, entrusted with the gospel, and appointed for ministry, Paul felt that he was *already* approved by God (1 Thess. 2:4; 1 Tim. 1:12). Resting secure in that divine affirmation is what enabled him to face the rejection of others.[4] Since he had the Spirit, he did not lose heart (2 Cor. 4:1).

---

4 Ajith Fernando lists many dangers for insecure leaders who are desperate for others' approval. See Fernando, *Jesus Driven Ministry*, 58.

However, having that confidence—even a measure of confidence in the Corinthians themselves—did not lead Paul to become passive or complacent in his approach toward them. Because, as he observed in their own lives, not everyone who claims the Spirit is spiritual (1 Cor. 3:1). Not everyone who exercises spiritual gifts has spiritual discernment. And, as it concerns Paul's opponents in Corinth, not everyone who boasts in ministry accomplishments or missionary fruit has reason to be confident. Such confidence is only for those who faithfully teach God's word and see others, by his Spirit, continue in righteousness, faithfulness, and a commitment to the true gospel.

Teaching the Spiritual

In spring 2018, I traveled to a remote part of Tanzania on the outskirts of Serengeti National Park. Another colleague and I were there teaching pastors and church leaders from various denominations. His group was studying Mark's Gospel while mine worked through Galatians.

Galatians is probably Paul's punchiest epistle. In it he wrestles rhetorically with a group of churches which he helped to establish on his first and second missionary journeys. The occasion for Paul's writing was that, to his dismay, the Galatian believers had quickly deserted him and were turning to a different gospel (Gal. 1:6). Intruders had infiltrated the church, encouraging Gentiles to be circumcised in keeping with the law of Moses. They were, according to Paul, propagating a false gospel and thus deserving of God's judgment (Gal. 1:7–9). Conversely, Paul argues that the promised Holy Spirit comes by faith in Christ, not through keeping the law. Therefore, Gentiles shouldn't be obligated to retroactively receive circumcision or obey Sinai's commands in order to be bona fide members of Christ's church.

As my class sat under a tarpaulin tent roof sheltering us from the sun, we considered Paul's line of reasoning in the letter. For the first two days, the students were tracking well. Then, when our study came to the third chapter of Galatians, I read aloud Paul's probing question: "Did you receive the Spirit by works of the law or by hearing with faith?" (Gal. 3:2). Somewhat hesitantly, a smattering of voices responded, "By hearing with faith." However, just as I was poised to proceed, one pastor raised his hand to challenge the consensus. "How can that be right?" he questioned. "We receive the Spirit by obeying God's commands."

Suffice it to say, the next thirty minutes of class didn't go as planned. First, I tried to understand his opinion. Then I tried to make Paul's argument—and his gospel—explicitly clear. From my perspective, our study of Galatians would be significantly hampered if we weren't on the same page regarding this foundational question. However, in the end, I'm not sure he was convinced. To this day, I'm not sure if he accurately grasped the gospel.

As troubling as that reality is, it's made worse by the knowledge that he was a pastor. This wasn't a random comment from a parishioner or layman, but the honest musings of an experienced shepherd of sheep. If he was misled, he would also mislead others. Sadly, such serious misunderstandings are not as unusual as you might imagine. That same week, my colleague had to address a different yet similarly egregious misinterpretation from the Gospel of Mark. One man in his class interpreted the story of Jesus's anointing at Bethany to suggest that all women should similarly serve and sacrifice for him, their spiritual leader.

In my travels around the world, I sometimes encounter local church leaders such as these with beliefs that are clearly false. Some might go so far as to label those church leaders as false teachers.

But I'm convinced that it's often a scenario where genuine, faithful Christians lack biblical instruction and sound theological training. Today, in many places where the gospel is spreading the fastest and where churches are rapidly multiplying, Satan appears to be the most active in deceiving believers. Simply having the Holy Spirit and the Bible does not guarantee a mature disciple.

This is one reason why I'm so concerned with the growing number of missionary strategies that advocate for the gospel's advance by reducing the amount of biblical instruction missionaries give new converts. Simplicity, it is argued, leads to reproducibility. Complicated teaching can't be easily or quickly transmitted. And since we've assumed that our ultimate goal is multiplication—and ideally, rapid growth—then the attendant means must be simple and transferable. Accordingly, missionaries are told to intentionally limit the content of doctrinal instruction to the irreducible core, focusing on obedience to the text at hand and its transference to others.[5]

However, discipleship is not that simple. The content of Paul's instruction to young believers and churches was incredibly broad and practical. He wasn't focused simply on transference or reproduction. Furthermore, he didn't prioritize obedience over knowledge. Instead, he was constantly concerned with an accurate understanding and application of the gospel, which led to Spirit-filled transformation. Paul provided us with neither an implicit example or an explicit command to simplify teaching as a strategic move to maximize reproduction. If anything, Paul's instruction to young believers and fledgling churches, as evidenced in his epistles, was relatively dense and complex. It was meaty.

---

5   A variety of methodologies focus on simplicity for the sake of reproducibility. One example is Obedience-Based Discipleship (OBD). For an analysis of this approach, see Zane Pratt, "Obedience-Based Discipleship," *Global Missiology* 4, no. 12 (July 2015).

In the case of Corinth, however, Paul lamented their lack of spiritual discernment, which limited him to basic principles. Milk, not solid food, was for those who were unspiritual (1 Cor. 3:1–2).[6] As long as the Corinthians were judging people by human standards and dividing along party lines, they weren't demonstrating themselves as spiritual, as truly understanding the gospel. Therefore, Paul couldn't teach them in the way he desired.

But for some reason, the dominant approach advocated by missiologists today seems to be anything but the Pauline method. For most missionaries, simple teaching isn't a concession, it's the strategic ideal. Since new believers have the Spirit, we assume that we need to provide them only with pablum, the equivalent of a mother's milk.[7] But Paul applied a contrary model. For those who had the Spirit, who showed themselves to be spiritual, he supplied more hearty instruction (1 Cor. 2:13). Paul's goal wasn't mere reproduction, but spiritual maturity and gospel fidelity. He wouldn't resign his influence among weak believers or a young church simply because they had God's word and God's Spirit.

The Inevitability of Influence

More than a century ago, Roland Allen wrote his influential *Missionary Methods: St. Paul's or Ours?* in which he concluded, "Now if we are to practise any methods approaching to the Pauline methods in power and directness, it is absolutely necessary that we should

6 "Interestingly, Paul reckoned it was in order for new believers to be given 'meat' as well as 'milk', but not at Corinth. They were not ready for it, even some years on from their conversion to Christ. 'Mere lapse of time does not bring Christian maturity' (Barrett)." See David Prior, *The Message of 1 Corinthians: Life in the Local Church* (Downers Grove, IL: IVP, 1985), 56.

7 In some versions of Disciple-Making Movements (DMM), missionaries encourage or expect *nonbelievers* to interpret, apply, obey, and teach the Bible *apart from* the indwelling Spirit.

first have this faith, this Spirit."[8] Specifically, Allen was challenging the prevailing missionary methods of his day. Rather than continue in the colonialist and paternalistic tendencies which he observed in North China, India, and East Africa, missionaries needed to adopt Paul's method of trusting national believers by trusting the Holy Spirit's work in them.

In the New Testament era, Allen argued, indigenous churches flourished as Paul released new congregations without trying to control their governance or micromanage their practice. Instead, he empowered them. "He gave as a right to the Spirit-bearing body the powers which duly belong to a Spirit-bearing body. He gave freely, and then he retired from them that they might learn to exercise the powers which they possessed in Christ."[9] This was key to a self-supporting, self-governing, and self-propagating national church.

At the time, Allen's perspective was a needed corrective. And the positive ripple effects from his emphasis on the Spirit can still be observed in mission strategy today. Our methods are now focused more than ever before on helping locals to reach their own peoples, lead their own ministries, and contextualize an indigenous theology, all while seeking to limit dependence on foreign resources and avoid any semblance of a foreign culture.

While there is much to commend about those goals, I fear that the legitimate concerns about cultural colonialism and dependency have also led some to overcompensate.[10] From my observations,

8 Roland Allen, *Missionary Methods: St. Paul's or Ours?* (Grand Rapids, MI: Eerdmans, 1962), 152.

9 Allen, *Missionary Methods*, 149.

10 For an early example, see Kaj Baago, "The Post-Colonial Crisis of Missions," *International Review of Mission* 55, no. 219 (July 1966), 322–32. For a more recent discussion, see Kay Higuera Smith, Jayachitra Lalitha, and L. Daniel Hawk, eds., *Evangelical Postcolonial Conversations: Global Awakenings in Theology and Praxis* (Downers Grove, IL: IVP, 2014).

missionaries from the West are now suspicious of the role of an outside teacher exercising influence over a national believer or congregation. In our efforts to develop churches in other cultures that are self-sustaining and self-governing, we've somehow felt the need to diminish our own selves—including the stewardship of our training and gifting—and God's purpose for us in that place. In such cases, we're confronting a new hazard in global missions. It's the danger of false humility and cultural embarrassment.

Instead of elevating the foreign worker, we now minimize the role of the Western missionary and emphasize the superiority of nationals. "They can do ministry better than we can" is the mantra of our day. And our primary objective is now seen as "empowerment," equipping locals while we serve from the shadows and prevent any sort of Western imposition. But I think this represents a departure from Allen's thesis,[11] and certainly from Paul's method.

Take, for example, Paul's work in Corinth. As a Jew from Cilicia, he had arrived as a cultural outsider. Yet he didn't merely call Greek converts to follow Jesus. He tells them, "Be imitators of me, as I am of Christ" (see 1 Cor. 4:16; 11:1). We should note here the nuance of the apostle's methodology. As we saw in chapter 1, he intentionally avoided creating followers of himself if it would elevate his reputation in a worldly way of one-upmanship. Yet in that same Corinthian context, Paul repeatedly calls local believers, as he does those in other churches, to follow him (1 Cor. 4:17). He is even willing to boast in his unique authority for establishing and building up the Corinthian church (2 Cor. 10:8). That doesn't mean Paul actively undermined local leadership. But when

---

11 See Allen, *Missionary Methods*, 147. See also J. D. Payne, "Roland Allen's *Missionary Methods* at One Hundred," in *Paul's Missionary Methods: In His Time and Ours*, eds. Robert L. Plummer and John Mark Terry (Downers Grove, IL: IVP, 2012), 235–43.

necessary—especially when they were going astray—he also didn't hesitate to correct them or send foreign representatives to implement his teaching. In the worst-case scenario, Paul was prepared to personally revisit them and resort to severe rebuke (1 Cor. 4:21; 2 Cor. 13:10).

This, then, presents us with a conundrum. Was Paul careful to limit his influence among new believers and churches on certain occasions or for certain reasons? Absolutely. Did he also withdraw from a place, entrusting national believers to the Spirit and thereby foster indigenous leadership? Yes. But Paul also insisted that new congregations follow his instruction and example, sometimes increasing his influence among them. He even continued his indirect oversight after he was gone. Of course, Paul was aware of cultural barriers and the need to be sensitive when working among people different than himself. But that difference didn't relegate him to the role of a mere supporting actor. As demonstrated in Corinth, Paul could lead from the front, from the side, or from far away.[12] He wanted them to follow him.[13]

Lesslie Newbigin, a strong critic of colonialist tendencies, recognized something of this challenge and the complicated nature of missionary influence. In keeping with Allen, he pleaded for "a recognition of the sovereignty and freedom of the Holy Spirit to bring the word of God in Jesus Christ to the consciences of men in his own way." Newbigin was concerned about missionary overreach and evangelists creating followers in their own ethical and cultural image. And yet, he realized, we are self-deceived if we think we can

---

12 One of the Corinthian complaints about Paul was the forcefulness of his influence when he was away from them (2 Cor. 10:10).

13 Some might argue that Paul's influence and authority were unique to his role as an apostle. However, that doesn't account for his advocacy of the authoritative teaching and example of an outsider like Timothy in Ephesus (1 Tim. 4:11–12) or Titus in Crete (Titus 2:1, 7).

somehow abstract the messenger from the message. The Jesus that people hear—and the Jesus they follow—is often the Jesus they see reflected in the missionary. "Even in preaching Christ [missionaries] will be, knowingly or unknowingly, advocating their own beliefs about what is good and true and desirable."[14]

It is practically impossible to remove external influence from the equation of cross-cultural ministry. To do so is to cease to be a missionary. The solution for our past failures—converting people to a culture rather than to Christ—is not to diminish the missionary's role to one of mere enablement. In fact, it's a Western myth to think that we can somehow equip and empower national believers without authoritatively communicating truth, modeling specific behavior, or even imposing certain values. In my experience, the very approach of "leading from behind" is an extremely Western concept which is baffling to many cultures. To adopt it as a strategy can itself become a form of foreign cultural imposition. Therefore, we must recognize that some measure of influence will always be inevitable. The critical question for Western missionaries in a postcolonial world isn't necessarily "How do we limit our influence?" Instead, it's better to ask, "Are we influencing others in the right way?"

Judging by the Flesh

That still leaves us with a central aspect of Allen's proposal and Paul's method of trusting locals by entrusting them to the Spirit. Specifically, I want to consider the question Did Paul's confidence in the Spirit lead him to be confident in the Corinthians? The answer, so far as I can tell, is yes and no.

---

14 Lesslie Newbigin, *The Open Secret: An Introduction to the Theology of Mission* (Grand Rapids, MI: Eerdmans, 1995), 138.

As is probably clear from our reflections thus far, Paul frequently oscillated between hopeful confidence and exasperated defense in his relationship with the Corinthians. Because of this, commentators often struggle to discern the exact situation in Corinth. Specifically regarding 2 Corinthians, many interpreters have observed a sharp distinction between Paul's encouraging tone in the first nine chapters and his firm warnings of the last four (2 Cor. 10–13). As a result, some have suggested that what we have in 2 Corinthians is a compilation of two or more Pauline letters. Others believe it was a single letter.[15] A third possibility is that Paul composed 2 Corinthians over a period of time (and travel) wherein he learned disheartening news that called the earlier good report from Titus into question.[16]

But however we might reconcile Paul's wide-ranging emotions and rhetorical approach in the Corinthian correspondence, it's clear that he had mixed feelings about them—as they did of him. In fact, of the many themes that are consistent throughout 2 Corinthians, one is that Paul was concerned the Corinthians were misunderstanding him. Some of them were judging him according to the flesh.

From the opening of the epistle, Paul boasts that he did not conduct his ministry "by earthly wisdom" (literally "fleshly wisdom"), "but by the grace of God" (2 Cor. 1:12). He does not make his plans "according to the flesh" (2 Cor. 1:17). This represents a direct challenge to those who suspect Paul of "walking according to the flesh" (2 Cor. 10:2). However, as Paul points out, his opponents

---

15 This is the view taken in this book. For a defense of the literary unity of the letter, see Paul Barnett, *The Second Epistle to the Corinthians* (Grand Rapids, MI: Eerdmans, 1997), 15–25.

16 D. A. Carson, *A Model of Christian Maturity: An Exposition of 2 Corinthians 10–13* (Grand Rapids, MI: Baker, 2019), 27–31. Paul's mixture of confidence and correction could also be the result of addressing multiple Achaian congregations in a single document.

were the ones who in fact judge people by outward appearances (2 Cor. 5:12).[17]

But by judging Paul by merely human standards—especially in their disdain for his weakness and suffering—the Corinthians demonstrated that they didn't truly understand the gospel. They didn't understand Christ.[18] According to Paul, the cross had toppled the worldly way of wisdom and human evaluation. "From now on, therefore, we regard no one according to the flesh. Even though we once regarded Christ according to the flesh, we regard him thus no longer" (2 Cor. 5:16). The problem with the Corinthians was not simply that they were turning against Paul. Their fleshly method of evaluation revealed a deeper problem: an inability to internalize the inverted values of the gospel. They didn't have the mind of Christ (1 Cor. 2:16).[19] Consequently, they were still evaluating human leaders by sight and not by faith. This was their perennial problem (1 Cor. 3:1–4).

Which brings us back to our question: Did Paul trust the Corinthians? At times he seems to have expressed a significant amount of confidence in them (2 Cor. 2:3; 7:16; cf. 8:22). However, Paul's words of confidence are better understood as rhetorical devices and a means of encouragement rather than unequivocal claims about his

17 "Ironically, they were charging Paul with living according to worldly standards that were not up to their own level of spiritual worth, whereas in reality they had so misunderstood the gospel that their own values were truly worldly, according to the 'flesh.'" See Carson, *Model of Christian Maturity*, 56.

18 See the helpful discussion of this problem in C. K. Barrett, *The Second Epistle to the Corinthians* (London: A & C Black, 1986), 48–49.

19 "Paul endorses the Corinthian catchphrase that people of the Spirit sift out everything, while no one else puts spiritual persons on trial or sifts them out (2:15)! However, for Paul the test of whether people are truly 'of the Spirit' is whether the Spirit has formed within them the mind-set of Christ (2:16)." See Anthony C. Thiselton, *The First Epistle to the Corinthians* (Grand Rapids, MI: Eerdmans, 2000), 286.

absolute assuredness. Just as he did in his Galatian letter, Paul could express confidence (Gal. 5:10) alongside significant concern (Gal. 3:1). In both Galatians and 2 Corinthians, Paul is deeply alarmed and positively hopeful at the same time. Furthermore, whatever confidence Paul does have in the Corinthians doesn't render him passive in the missionary task, but urges him to write, to visit, and to challenge their misunderstandings and misapplications of his teaching. Consider this appeal from Paul as he begins the final section of 2 Corinthians and prepares for his third visit:

> I beg of you that when I am present I may not have to show boldness with such confidence as I count on showing against some who suspect us of walking according to the flesh. For though we walk in the flesh, we are not waging war according to the flesh. For the weapons of our warfare are not of the flesh but have divine power to destroy strongholds. We destroy arguments and every lofty opinion raised against the knowledge of God, and take every thought captive to obey Christ, being ready to punish every disobedience, when your obedience is complete. (2 Cor. 10:2–6)

Those aren't the words of apostolic complacency or blind confidence. Those aren't the words of a servant in the shadows or a cheerleader from the sidelines. But also note, those aren't the words of a missionary depending on human means and fleshly wisdom. To rely on the Spirit, according to Paul, is to wage war against wrong opinions, false understandings, and human pride with the weapons of righteousness (2 Cor. 6:7). To make disciples who obey all that Jesus commanded can and does include the necessary work of correcting the disobedience of faulty faith. Paul isn't just concerned with right actions; he's concerned with right thinking, right knowing, and right believing.

In all this, Paul wants to encourage the Corinthians. He is hoping for the best—looking forward to their complete obedience. But that doesn't mean that Paul completely trusts them. In fact, he can't. Why? Perhaps most importantly, because he doesn't know for sure if they truly possess the Spirit and are spiritual. He doesn't know if they have true, saving faith (2 Cor. 13:5; cf. 2 Cor. 5:20). Like Paul, they need to acquire a "second way of seeing."[20] They need to live by faith rather than sight (2 Cor. 5:7). They need to fix their eyes on the unseen rather than the seen, "to see the events of this age in the light of the age to come."[21] They need to be able to look "beyond the earthen jar to the treasure within."[22] Rather than judge according to the flesh, they need to judge all things by the Spirit.

Ministry of Righteousness by the Spirit

Recently I spoke with a missionary who works among an unreached people group in North Africa. During our conversation, he shared with me his concern regarding what seems to him to be the common missiological strategy among all organizations in his region—if not all the world. In his words, the principles of simplicity and reproducibility have become the twin guard rails that keep mission strategy

---

20 Nijay Gupta highlights this aspect of faith specifically in 2 Corinthians, but also in the broader New Testament (John 20:29; 2 Cor. 5:7; Heb. 11:1; 1 Pet. 1:8). "This is what we call *believing faith*, faith that can believe the unbelievable and 'see' what is unseen because the eyes have been trained to *look* for the right things. Glory is not found in the flamboyant exterior but the density, determination, and weightiness of the soul and will. Honor is not about the absence of scars, but the interpretation of vicarious scars as reflective of a noble heart." See Nijay Gupta, *Paul and the Language of Faith* (Grand Rapids, MI: Eerdmans, 2020), 133.

21 Barrett, *The Second Epistle to the Corinthians*, 34.

22 John B. Polhill, *Paul and His Letters* (Nashville: B&H, 1999), 270.

on the straight and narrow. If your discipleship is simple and your disciples are reproducing, you know you're doing the right thing.

Specifically, he expressed frustration from his many conversations with other missionaries about discipleship models and content that focus simply on obedience. In his experience, the gospel is easily obscured by such methods. And he's concerned by Muslims he's seen who, when coming to Christ, are simply converting to a different system of works. They may pray differently. They may give differently. They may even elevate the commands of Jesus and pass them on to others. But they're simply continuing in a modification of the same works-based religion. They've mastered obedience. But he wonders if they know Christ. He's not sure they have the Spirit.

Further complicating the situation, whenever this missionary has tried to have meaningful dialogue with colleagues about these troubling observations, he's run into the roadblock of results. From their perspective, this approach works. The gospel—at least as they understand it—is advancing. Disciples are being made. Groups are gathering. And since these other missionaries are "seeing results," his questions and challenges are dismissed as either overly arrogant or unnecessarily critical.

One of the strangest axioms I've heard from missionaries over the years is, "You can't argue with results." If something works, don't question it. When a ministry or a methodology is bringing people to Jesus and bearing fruit, then it's clearly good and from God. Consequently, growth and reproduction aren't simply understood as the ultimate goal of missions; they're now the standard by which ministries are evaluated and new strategies are developed.[23]

---

23 An example of this is the development of CPM strategy based on observations and field research. See David Garrison, *Church Planting Movements: How God Is Redeeming a Lost World* (Midlothian, VA: WIGTake Resources, 2004).

But seeing results isn't everything. Take, for example, Paul's opponents at Corinth. They were missionaries who clearly boasted in the product of their work (2 Cor. 5:12). They viewed themselves as apostles of Christ and servants of righteousness (2 Cor. 11:13–15). Yet Paul called them out for judging merely by outward appearance, living according to the flesh, and encouraging obedience to God's law that didn't emanate from an accurate understanding of the gospel.[24] They were leading people to the Scriptures and to Moses, but theirs was a different Jesus, a different gospel, and a different spirit (2 Cor. 11:4). So whatever boast they were making was based on a purely superficial evaluation. The righteousness of their disciples, according to Paul, wasn't the righteousness that comes by faith as the fruit of the Spirit. Therefore, it was perfectly appropriate for him to argue with their results.

For Paul, the ultimate question isn't whether there are visible products to someone's ministry, but whether or not those results are born by the Spirit. According to Paul, what makes his new covenant ministry so glorious is the presence of the Spirit. The law of Moses had a measure of glory, but it was passing. The Spirit brought permanent glory through an internal change of the heart that resulted in the genuine fruit of enduring righteousness. Apart from the life-giving work of the Holy Spirit in someone's life, mere commands only produce condemnation and death (2 Cor. 3:4–11).

Central to Paul's defense of his new covenant ministry is the reality that, through the Spirit, true righteousness was being revealed (cf. Rom. 3:21). That righteousness was objectively found in the

24 Barnett understands Paul's opponents to be Judaizers whose "purpose in coming to Corinth was to 'minister' the 'righteousness' associated with Moses and the law ('on tablets of stone . . . the letter'—3:3, 6), as opposed to the 'righteousness' issuing in 'reconciliation with God' based on Christ's death (3:9; 5:21), which was the 'ministry' of Paul (3:6; cf. 2:17–3:4; 5:18, 19, 20)." See Barnett, *The Second Epistle to the Corinthians*, 35.

work of Jesus who lived a life of full obedience and gave himself as a substitute for sinners, the righteous for the unrighteous (2 Cor. 5:21; cf. 1 Pet. 3:18). This good news is the foundation for all our obedience. But the Christian life of righteousness isn't merely started by faith and the Spirit, with the flesh pulling us across the finish line (Gal. 3:3). Spiritual transformation from beginning to end, along with increasing conformity to the image of God, takes place through the ongoing act of beholding the glory of God in the gospel (2 Cor. 3:18).[25] Growth in grace happens through faith in Jesus and the sanctifying presence of the Spirit such that new covenant believers demonstrate the harvest of abiding righteousness in their lives (2 Cor. 9:10).

The contrast here is crucial. Paul's opponents were also calling for righteousness or obedience. But obedience to what end? And righteousness by what means? Paul didn't quibble with whether or not their ministries were "fruitful"; he challenged whether they were faithful.

If my missionary friend from North Africa is correct, then a version of that old Corinthian problem is still a danger in much of the world today. The call to make disciples isn't merely a call to make sure people obey God's word. And our missionary ambition cannot simply be a strategy of reproduction. Even if we see growth—with field research showing obvious multiplication—we must not evaluate ministries merely by outward appearances or mission practices by worldly values. We must not judge according to the flesh.

The letter of recommendation for every missionary and their hope of one day receiving God's commendation are found in the visible results of lives transformed by the invisible Spirit, not merely

---

25 "The effect of continuous beholding is that we are continuously being transformed." See Hughes, *Paul's Second Epistle to the Corinthians*, 118.

evidenced in conversion, but in those who continue in righteousness and reject falsehood. That is our aim. But we must also recognize the means of that mission. The sanctifying work of the Spirit takes place in all of us as we behold the glory of the Lord reflected in the face of Jesus. Gazing upon the gospel—not just committing to obey—is how we are increasingly changed into his image from one degree of glory to another (2 Cor. 3:18).[26] Just as Paul was transformed by his heavenly vision, believers are radically remade as they look upon the glory of Jesus through the eyes of faith.

Looking to Glory

Sadly, as James O. Fraser observed from his ministry among the Lisu, "Much Christian work seems to have the stamp of the carnal upon it. It may be 'good,' it may be successful outwardly—but the Shekinah Glory is not there."[27] Fraser's goal was to see that kind of glory. To my knowledge, few missionaries have exemplified dependence on the Spirit as much as he did.

In 1915, some seven years after his arrival in China, Fraser wrote to supporters in an extended letter pleading with them to join him in earnest prayer. He had seen only a handful of the Lisu turn from idols to serve the living God. He was desperate for the Spirit's power. So he asked each of them to set apart some time each day ("say half an hour or so?") for prayer.[28] Together with them, he labored in intercession. Meanwhile, the lack of converts was driving him to

26 This implies that there are degrees of glory now for the Christian who, seeing Jesus, is transformed into the same image and experiences increased glory. See Barrett, *The Second Epistle to the Corinthians*, 125.

27 As quoted in Taylor, *Behind the Ranges*, 129.

28 Taylor, *Behind the Ranges*, 135. After a season of amazing harvest, Fraser was concerned that his converts "were quite indifferent to anything beyond the first elements of Christian truth." Thus, he committed to provide them with greater instruction. "My mistake has too often been that of too much haste." See Taylor, *Behind the Ranges*, 188–89.

bouts of depression. Within the year, Fraser considered abandoning his post. However, in a last-ditch effort, he decided to return for a final time to preach in some of the mountain villages in Yunnan Province. Then, just as he was prepared to leave, God turned his farewell tour into a victory lap. In answer to years of importunate prayer, scores of households turned to Christ in what was the beginning of a decades-long harvest.

In a sermon entitled "The Lord's Work in the Lord's Way," Francis Schaeffer once identified what he believed to be "the *central* problem of our age." The primary threat to Christians and ministries is "tending to do the Lord's work in the power of the flesh rather than of the Spirit."[29] As he saw it, the church is in constant need of remembering her weakness and her desperate need for God's strength. Schaeffer, therefore, called us to humility and dependence.

> Is it not amazing: Though we know the power of the Holy Spirit can be ours, we still ape the world's wisdom, trust its forms of publicity, its noise, and imitate its ways of manipulating men! If we try to influence the world by using its methods, we are doing the Lord's work in the flesh. If we put activity, even good activity, at the center rather than trusting God, then there may be the power of the world but we will lack the power of the Holy Spirit.[30]

Perhaps surprisingly, Schaeffer also connected the virtue of humility with our desire for God's approval. Those who know that their works will one day be tried by God are those who live for his affirmation and praise. This reality doesn't make us proud or ar-

---

29 Francis A. Schaeffer, *No Little People* (Downers Grove, IL: IVP, 1977), 64.

30 Schaeffer, *No Little People*, 69.

rogant, relying on our own strength. Just the opposite. Knowledge of God's judgment causes us to cast ourselves on his mercy and depend on his Spirit. For only then will we have the hope of God's approving word for our work.

For the apostle Paul, the hope of success in his ambassadorial ministry wasn't his pedigree, education, or work ethic. He put no confidence in the flesh. Rather, his confidence was in the permanent glory of the Spirit producing changed lives by the gospel. His ministry in Corinth was validated by the Spirit's work among the faithful there. Therefore, as the thorn had taught him, Paul needed to constantly rely on the Spirit.

But his dependence on God's power didn't render Paul passive. It made him extremely active, seeking to construct the Corinthians' faith by dismantling faulty opinions and false gospels. Having received the down payment of future glory didn't make Paul self-confident or complacent; it made him seek greater glory.

The question for any missionary who desires to follow Paul's example is: How can we be confident of God's affirming word if we create followers apart from the Spirit? Furthermore, how can we expect God's approval if we release to the Spirit those who are living by the flesh? If we aren't willing to teach or tear down, to break apart and build up, how will we know that what we construct is secure on the foundation of Christ?[31] How can we be confident to receive a reward (1 Cor. 3:14)?

While Paul was clearly assured by the Holy Spirit's presence within him—reflecting the glory of God like the glowing of Moses's face—he still recognized a test was one day coming. God's initial approval by setting him apart for ministry didn't mean that Paul's

---

31 Jeremiah was commissioned to uproot and break down, to build and to plant (Jer. 1:10; 31:28). Paul employed these two metaphors for his ministry in Corinth (1 Cor. 3:6, 10).

missionary efforts were sure to pass the exam (1 Thess. 2:4). Paul's heavenly vision and the confidence of the resurrection didn't lead to a glorious resignation; it produced in him a sobering hope. So, whether he was at home or away—caught up to paradise or back in Cilicia—he made it his aim to please God and persuade others (2 Cor. 5:6–10). And the only way any of us can hope to do the same is through the power of the Spirit.

5

Speaking the Truth Sincerely

Miletus

WORD ARRIVED BY COURIER to the church in Ephesus. Their peripatetic apostle was sailing along the sawtooth shore of Asia Minor and had docked at Miletus. He wished to see them, but time was scarce. Paul was en route to Jerusalem and couldn't afford the inevitable delay of a personal visit to his beloved congregation—not to mention the threat of arrest. He requested a delegation of Ephesian elders to make the seventy-kilometer trek southward to say goodbye. This was his last chance to see them.

Some five years earlier, Paul charted a similar course that began in Corinth and headed eastward. At that time, he made an abbreviated stop in Ephesus, leaving behind Aquila and Priscilla to work there. Together with Apollos, they spoke fervently and accurately about Jesus among the Jewish diaspora such that, a year later, when Paul returned after strengthening the churches in Galatia, he found an active community of believers in Ephesus (Acts 18:27). And Paul chose to stay.

During his three years in Ephesus, Luke tells us that Paul spent the first few months speaking boldly in the synagogue, "persuading them about the kingdom of God" (Acts 19:8). But when that opportunity turned into opposition, he moved his operation to the hall of Tyrannus where he reasoned daily with all who would listen. As a result, the word of the Lord spread throughout Asia Minor, including the prominent port city of Miletus (Acts 19:10).

Despite what he described as a wide door for work in Ephesus, Paul's years there were some of the most difficult. It was from Ephesus that the apostle composed his first Corinthian letter, reporting to the churches in Achaia that his ministry of proclamation was being met by many adversaries (1 Cor. 16:9). Later, Paul wrote to the Corinthians about another severe experience of affliction in Asia, opaquely referring to events that led him to extreme despair (2 Cor. 1:8).

While the Corinthians may have received limited information about his suffering, the Ephesian elders were eyewitness to Paul's sorrow. Sharing in his sufferings produced a camaraderie stronger than the bonds of mere friendship. If this was to be their final farewell, a mere seventy kilometers wouldn't separate them. So they traveled to Miletus, no doubt anticipating an emotional departure.

For whatever else they expected from that poignant send-off, Paul left them with a moving and unforgettable speech (Acts 20:17–38). He charged them to remember and replicate his pattern of life among them, specifically his faithful preaching and personal integrity. Paul recounted for them how he was humble during trials and worked hard in his tentmaking. Paul rehearsed how, in spite of incredible danger, he didn't shrink back from proclaiming the kingdom, declaring the whole counsel of God, and admonishing with tears—how he did so in public venues and private homes both night and day for three years. He called them, as ministers of the gospel and shepherds of God's flock, to do likewise.

Anyone who would emulate Paul's missionary method must take this farewell address for what it is: the self-described pattern of the apostle set forward as the self-conscious model for all Christian ministry. Apostles, evangelists, shepherds, and elders are those who boldly proclaim the good news of Jesus through a lifestyle that adorns and accords with that same gospel. Christ's ambassadors are those who speak the truth with sincerity.

Open Statement of the Truth

When missionary Henry Martyn completed his magisterial translation of the New Testament into the Persian language in February of 1812, he commissioned local artisans to produce two copies in the finest script. His plan was to formally present his work to the Shah for approval. By May, the books were ready. But Martyn needed a way to reach the Shah. He decided to recruit the support and influence of the British ambassador located in Tabriz. The problem was that seven hundred miles separated Martyn, in Shiraz to the south, from the ambassador in the far northwest of Persia. And Martyn was seriously ill.

A month later, Martyn reached the halfway point in Tehran, though he wasn't sure he should continue. Instead of prolonging his misery and delaying his mission, he opted for a more direct route. The Shah's summer campground was only a few miles from Tehran, so Martyn made arrangements for a personal appeal. Armed with letters of recommendation, he approached the Shah's vizier. After a positive first interview with two secretaries of state, Martyn was invited back. This time, he faced more hours of scrutiny, debating with multiple Muslim scholars.

Eventually, having heard the disputed doctrines of the Christian missionary, the vizier presented a demand: "You had better say 'God is God, and Muhammad is the prophet of God.'" In the words of Martyn's biographer, "It was a straight challenge to accept the Muslim creed; there could be only one answer, however disastrous the consequences to his mission." Later reflecting on how he responded in that tenuous moment, Martyn recalled, "I said, 'God is God,' but instead of adding 'Muhammad is the prophet of God,' I said, 'and Jesus is the Son of God.'"[1]

If there was ever a time to soft-pedal on theological conviction, that was it. Surrounded by opponents who could snuff out years of precious labor, not to mention his own life, Martyn was left with a decision. Presented with the opportunity to smooth surfaces with his interrogators, he provided what was perhaps the most abrasive answer possible. Not because he was bombastic, brusque, or unaccommodating. If anything, the English missionary was known for having a timid disposition, recoiling at the thought of personal confrontation. However, from earliest days Martyn also possessed an overriding and "vivid sense of responsibility" to deliver God's message.[2] This conviction led him to proclaim the gospel wherever he went, even at the threat of his own security.

The apostle Paul felt a similar responsibility. He viewed his apostolic ministry as a stewardship. God had entrusted him with the weighty responsibility of protecting and passing on his authoritative gospel as the ambassador of heaven. Whether with Jews or

1 Richard T. France, "Henry Martyn," in *Five Pioneer Missionaries* (Carlisle, PA: Banner of Truth, 1999), 291.
2 France, "Henry Martyn," 248.

Gentiles, women or men, Roman officials or Greek philosophers, Paul's method was essentially the same. On behalf of God, he boldly announced the resurrected and exalted Son of God who would one day return to judge the world. Through Paul, God was calling all people everywhere to repent (Acts 17:30).

If I were to distill the Pauline missionary method into one word, it would be *speaking*. Whereas the grace and power for Paul's ministry were derived by the Spirit, his manner of fulfilling God's commission was most basically communicative.[3] God had given him the ministry of reconciliation, so he appealed to others on behalf of God, imploring them to be reconciled to God through Christ (2 Cor. 5:20). He spoke the truth, doing so with passion, persuasion, authority, and reason.

Accordingly, when Silas and Timothy first arrived in Corinth, they found Paul "occupied with the word, testifying to the Jews that the Christ was Jesus" (Acts 18:5). Later, when the leaders of the synagogue openly rejected his message, Paul relocated to the house next door, continuing with his evangelistic emphasis. Around that time, the Lord appeared to him and urged Paul to "go on speaking and do not be silent" (Acts. 18:9). For eighteen months, he remained in Corinth, a period which Luke summarized by this singular act: "teaching the word of God among them" (Acts. 18:11). Later, when Paul reflected on his own arrival in Corinth, he similarly described his mission in terms of preaching the testimony of God (1 Cor. 2:1). Together with Silas and Timothy, Paul proclaimed Jesus Christ to be the Son of God

---

3 David Hesselgrave considers at length this communicative center of the cross-cultural witness. He highlights how this ambassadorial role is not merely one of teaching or instruction but of impassioned persuasion. See David J. Hesselgrave, *Communicating Christ Cross-Culturally: An Introduction to Missionary Communication* (Grand Rapids, MI: Zondervan, 1991), 84–85.

(2 Cor. 1:19). In fact, the entirety of his new covenant ministry could be characterized by this: the open statement of the truth (2 Cor. 4:2).[4]

Paul's remarkable boldness to preach the gospel was certainly owing to his confidence in its origins. He believed his message to be the very words of God. But Paul did not abstract the truthfulness of that message from the trustworthiness of its messenger. So when the Corinthians began to question Paul—about something as trivial as his fluctuating travel itinerary—he was concerned that they were ultimately questioning God. That is why he worked so hard to defend his reputation among the Corinthians. He wanted them to see that they could trust him in the same way they trusted God.[5]

From the outset of 2 Corinthians, then, Paul provided personal testimony to defend his integrity. He conducted his ministry with single-mindedness and sincerity (2 Cor. 1:12). His conscience was clear.[6] He made his plans with pure intentions, always doing what was best for their sake. Unlike the false teachers who were pandering to their desires, Paul didn't market God's word as a way to take advantage of them or advance his own cause. He along with Silas and Timothy were reliable men of honor. As Paul writes, defending

---

4 "*That* is the ministry of reconciliation [in 2 Cor. 5] Paul understands God to have given him—to 'appeal' to lost sinners and 'implore' them to 'be reconciled to God' (v. 20). It is not a ministry of partnering with God in his work of renewing the cosmos by confronting social problems." See Kevin DeYoung and Greg Gilbert, *What Is the Mission of the Church? Making Sense of Social Justice, Shalom, and the Great Commission* (Wheaton, IL: Crossway, 2011), 207.

5 This is the astonishing logic of 2 Cor. 1:15–22: If God is true, then so is Paul. Both the apostle's plans and his preaching express the faithfulness of God. See Paul Barnett, *The Second Epistle to the Corinthians* (Grand Rapids, MI: Eerdmans, 1997), 104–5.

6 "Paul's personal vindication of his own conscience is no light matter; it is done in the confidence of God's present and eschatological vindication of him." See Barnett, *The Second Epistle to the Corinthians*, 95.

his team, "We are not, like so many, peddlers of God's word, but as men of sincerity, as commissioned by God, in the sight of God we speak in Christ" (2 Cor. 2:17).[7]

For Paul, the twin values of public proclamation and personal reputation were inseparable in the defense of his apostolic ministry. In his first letter to the Thessalonians, the same two themes of bold preaching and pure motivation also emerge with striking emphasis. A large section of that letter, written from Corinth, is worth quoting here:

> For you yourselves know, brothers, that our coming to you was not in vain. But though we had already suffered and been shamefully treated at Philippi, as you know, we had boldness in our God to declare to you the gospel of God in the midst of much conflict. For our appeal does not spring from error or impurity or any attempt to deceive, but just as we have been approved by God to be entrusted with the gospel, so we speak, not to please man, but to please God who tests our hearts. For we never came with words of flattery, as you know, nor with a pretext for greed—God is witness. Nor did we seek glory from people, whether from you or from others, though we could have made demands as apostles of Christ. But we were gentle among you, like a nursing mother taking care of her own children. So, being affectionately desirous of you, we were ready to share with you not only the gospel of God but also our own selves, because you had become very dear to us.

---

7   Paul emphasized to the Corinthians that he conducted his ministry in God's sight or presence (2 Cor. 1:12, 23; 2:10, 17; 3:4; 4:2; 7:12; 8:21). He sought to face his Judge with a clear conscience (Acts 23:1; 24:15–16), even calling God as his witness (Rom. 1:9; 2 Cor. 1:23; 1 Thess. 2:5).

For you remember, brothers, our labor and toil: we worked night and day, that we might not be a burden to any of you, while we proclaimed to you the gospel of God. You are witnesses, and God also, how holy and righteous and blameless was our conduct toward you believers. For you know how, like a father with his children, we exhorted each one of you and encouraged you and charged you to walk in a manner worthy of God, who calls you into his own kingdom and glory. (1 Thess. 2:1–12)

Paul's ministry was fundamentally one of speaking. He boldly declared the gospel. He appealed to his hearers. He spoke to please God. He shared the gospel with others, exhorting, encouraging, and charging them.[8] But notice that Paul's bold speech was not simply based on the truthfulness of his message. True, Paul was convinced that he brought an authoritative word from God that was without error. But Paul's courageous appeal also arose out of the purity of his motives. He knew he wasn't tricking anyone by his testimony. He wasn't selling snake oil. He wasn't trying to make a buck, attempting to please people, or seeking their praise. Paul was able to boldly declare the gospel because he genuinely desired to serve them and please God. He knew himself to be sincere and trustworthy.

The Nonnegotiable of Missionary Integrity

I remember the first time I met my landlord in Central Asia. After the niceties of a cultural greeting, his initial question was, "So, you work for the CIA?" Taken aback, I replied in the negative while chuckling uncomfortably. He didn't laugh.

---

8   For a consideration of evangelistic proclamation as more than "sharing the gospel," see Elliot Clark, *Evangelism as Exiles: Life on Mission as Strangers in Our Own Land* (Austin, TX: The Gospel Coalition, 2019), 94.

Over the next several months, I began to realize that his question represented a wider assumption. He had verbalized an opinion that many of my neighbors shared: I had come to infiltrate their community and subvert their government. They had me pegged from day one. So it would be naïve to suppose that he or they would blindly accept my simple dismissal.[9]

In many places, missionaries are received, whether at customs or the local coiffeur, with suspicion. Their words are rarely believed. That's because more and more kingdom ambassadors are going into areas that are increasingly nationalistic or hostile to the gospel. Even when the locals aren't opposed to Christianity per se, they may simply distrust foreigners. As a result, many missionaries face an uphill climb for relational credibility.

Adding to this challenge, as missionaries go abroad—whether to a closed Muslim country or even a secular nation tightening borders—they're increasingly forced to use nontraditional means of obtaining entry and securing residency. Some go as tourists, others as students or teachers. Many operate an NGO or some other business. But few obtain religious worker visas. And herein lies the struggle—one that plays out in the innermost parts of a missionary's psyche. It's the stress of personal identity.

Who am I? I know I'm not a CIA agent. But what do I say when my neighbor, or the police, asks if I'm a missionary?

I've dealt with that question on many occasions. And I've witnessed my colaborers respond in various ways. They said they were authors, educators, developers, consultants, artists, and designers—

9 This section is adapted from an article originally published by The Gospel Coalition. See Elliot Clark, "The Non-Negotiable of Missionary Integrity," The Gospel Coalition (website), April 20, 2018, https://www.thegospelcoalition.org/.

just to name a few. In some cases, they were. But in others, they really weren't.

Sadly, some missionaries don't do *any* of the work they say they do. Or they do it so infrequently—or consistently operate their business in the red—that no one could ever hope to live on their salary, much less support a family. So whenever the question comes, "Where do you get your money?" they have no comfortable or forthright response. Some expats pack up and move their families halfway around the world, then tell their neighbors they aren't going to start work for a couple years until they've learned the language. I know, because that's what I did.

But our foreign neighbors can see right through this façade. Every other breadwinner in the community has a long work week while I seemingly do nothing. *What sinister work must he be plotting each day behind his computer and within the confines of his apartment?* I mean, wouldn't you be asking those same questions if a Saudi man brought his family to your neighborhood but didn't seem to work or have a source of income? And if you ever dared ask, what if he stuttered about some nebulous plan for the possibility of future employment?

So it is for many missionaries. They face the day-in-day-out dilemma of governmental scrutiny. But far more significant is the perception of the local community. It matters little what a pencil-pushing bureaucrat in the foreign office thinks. Missionaries must concern themselves first with their own occupational incongruity, which is of foremost concern to the family next door.

To be clear, I'm not suggesting these missionaries are lying. In fact, I think in most cases they're saying factual things. I'm also not opposed to using platforms, operating businesses, or starting an NGO. Provided they're legitimate and ethical, these are good means that have wonderful potential for creating opportunities for ministry, much like Paul's use of his tentmaking occupation. However, Paul didn't use his business just to gain access to a place or put bread on the table. His work was a means of demonstrating his personal credibility. Paul could point to his occupational integrity in defense of the gospel and as the source of his bold posture in evangelism. That's the missionary question. Are our businesses, identities, platforms, and projects ultimately credible? Or do we undermine the message we proclaim by being unbelievable ourselves?

Far too often we in the missionary community have focused on creating *access* without building *credibility*. We've been doing *business* without personal or organizational *integrity*. And as the buzz swirls in the missionary community around the trending model of business as mission—which I believe presents us with wonderful possibilities—we must acknowledge that it will work only if those involved actually do their business and do it well.

Such is the cost of modern missions. It may not mean persecution or martyrdom, even in the most dangerous locations. Instead, it may mean endless hours of humdrum labor to the glory of God. This is the nonnegotiable price of personal integrity in missions. We must recognize that people will trust our message only if they can trust its messenger. This is especially significant because we preach a message that depends on credibility. The gospel summons trust. So if missionaries forfeit personal integrity, they have essentially forfeited the ability to do their job. After all, if someone doesn't believe *you*, they'll never believe what you have to say.

Faithful Presence and Faithful Proclamation

In the remote Central Asian city where I used to live, missionary families from two different organizations worked together for the sake of the gospel. I led a small group committed to making Christ known primarily through a ministry of the word. We viewed *faithful proclamation* as central to mission. Meanwhile, the leader from the other organization stressed the importance of making Christ known through a ministry of deeds. He viewed *faithful presence* as central to mission.

This divide represents a not-so-subtle split among missionaries around the world today. Is our ministry incarnational (living like Christ) or representational (speaking for Christ)?[10] Are people drawn to the gospel by our way of life, or by the words we speak? Are we joining with God in the renewal of all things, or is our primary responsibility to proclaim the gospel and make disciples?

While those are complex questions, hopefully it's clear by now that I don't think we can ever pit our witness against our way of life. The message of the gospel is believable precisely because its messenger is similarly reliable.[11] However, we cannot shrink the missionary task to one of faithful presence, of *being Christ* to those around us. As Eckhard Schnabel argues, Paul describes his own missionary task as focusing *primarily* on the preaching of the gospel.[12] Furthermore, we must recognize that, in the Corinthian correspondence, Paul presents his proclamational priority as the

---

10 For a helpful discussion of this question, see the chapter on "Incarnationalism and Representationalism" in Hesselgrave, *Paradigms*, 141–63.

11 "Paul affirms that the trustworthiness of the message he proclaims is bound up with his own ethical behavior (2 Cor. 1:17–22). . . . The same God who validated and anointed Paul for ministry is the God who always stands true to his promises. If the messenger (Paul!) is flawed, then so is the message." See Thomas R. Schreiner, *Paul: Apostle of God's Glory in Christ* (Downers Grove, IL: IVP, 2001), 98.

12 Schnabel argues that, based on Paul's example, the primary missionary calling is to convey the good news publicly, "with divine authority and with courageous boldness." See Schnabel, "Paul the Missionary," in *Paul's Missionary Methods*, eds. Robert L. Plummer and John Mark Terry (Downers Grove, IL: IVP, 2012), 210–15.

model for all believers.[13] If we are to follow Paul's example, then the way we will fulfill the missionary mandate is first and foremost by *speaking of Christ*.

But this is not the way that many missionaries today conceive of their task. The missions community has largely abandoned a "proclamational model" for others deemed more effective and multiplicative.[14] Not only that, but many today eschew the very idea of following Paul as our model in the first place. Western workers are now encouraged to avoid the Pauline pattern. Instead, many talk of trying to be more like Barnabas—an encourager who succeeds as a supporting actor.

Recently I had a friendly email exchange with a missionary who serves in Greece. During our conversation, he articulated this approach as part of his larger CPM strategy. He didn't intend to follow Paul's example. In fact, he felt that following Paul's example leads to all kinds of problems. Instead, his explicit goal was to raise up local leaders who would themselves become like Paul. Meanwhile, he would seek to serve alongside them, more like Barnabas, allowing the locals to do the primary work of reaching their people and raising up other leaders.

On the face of it, the strategy sounds appealing. For one, how could any of us presume to be like Paul? Also, surely the locals are a step ahead culturally, better able to empathize and communicate with others in their community? However, it's troubling to me when we as missionaries expect a national to be someone we aren't and

---

13 Peter O'Brien argues in his chapter "Paul's Ambition and Ours" that Christians are called to more than simply an exemplary or winsome lifestyle. We should mimic Paul's ambition—in our own unique ways and giftings—"seeking by all means to save many." See Peter J. O'Brien, *Gospel and Mission in the Writings of Paul* (Grand Rapids, MI: Baker, 1995), 106.

14 For example, see the contrasting CPM model advocated for by Ted Esler, "Two Church Planting Paradigms," *International Journal of Frontier Missiology* 30, no. 2 (Summer 2013): 67–73.

to do something we won't. Furthermore, this methodology ignores the uncomfortable reality that Paul puts himself forward as the standard for us all. As seen in his speech at Miletus, Paul presents his personal integrity and proclamational priority as *the* authoritative example for what it means to be a minister of the gospel.[15]

Even as early as a century ago, Roland Allen recognized that missionaries were shrinking back from this Pauline model of preaching. In his estimation, the loss of missionary proclamation was owing to a loss in "two of the most prominent elements of St Paul's Gospel: the doctrine of the judgment at hand, and the doctrine of the wrath of God." Allen explained:

> St Paul did not preach that in times past men had lived under the stern dominion of law and that with the Gospel had come a day of toleration; he preached that in times past God had been longsuffering, and that now He called all men everywhere to repent, because the day of judgment was at hand.[16]

Because he recognized the fear of the Lord, Paul persuaded others (2 Cor. 5:11). He didn't passively wait for the Spirit or speak up only when he discerned that God was already at work. Paul didn't enter a city and delay preaching until he found a person of peace. He didn't defer to dreams and visions, only speaking with those already interested in Jesus.[17] Nor was Paul's

---

15 Also, while Paul seems to have been the "chief speaker" (Acts 14:12), it's untenable to assume that his companions, such as Barnabas, Silas, or Timothy, were not also actively involved in the ministry of teaching and preaching (Acts 13:1, 5, 43, 46; 14:1–3, 21, 25; 15:35–36; 16:10, 17, 31–33; cf. 2 Cor. 1:19).

16 Roland Allen, *Missionary Methods: St. Paul's or Ours?* (Grand Rapids, MI: Eerdmans, 1962), 72.

17 Lebanese pastor Hikmat Kashouh notes that our Christian witness rarely follows the Pauline method that was "passionate and proclamational," and he wonders if God would "have to

method to reluctantly submit personal opinions and defer to his hearers. He didn't facilitate self-discovery or promote group-led discussions of the Bible. If there wasn't a preacher, how could he be confident that the lost would believe and be saved (Rom. 10:14)? Without a teacher, how would they understand (cf. Acts 8:31)?

Therefore, the apostle spoke the truth boldly. As the herald of good news (Isa. 40:9–11; 52:7), he announced God's word with authority and conviction, calling his hearers to respond. In the words of Allen, Paul didn't broadly scatter seeds; he planted.[18] By that, Allen meant that Paul demanded his hearers make a choice. If in the end they rejected him, he knew they were rejecting God. If his gospel was veiled, it was veiled because the god of this world had blinded the minds of the perishing. But the divinely appointed means for opening those blind eyes and revealing the glory of God was through the foolishness of preaching. The way to *see* the light was by *hearing* the word (2 Cor. 4:1–6).

Since Paul was confident in this glorious work of the Spirit through his frail human body, he boldly preached the gospel. He did not lose heart. If his confidence waned, he would have stopped preaching. He would have surrendered the central task of his missionary call. But Paul didn't, because he couldn't. Along with his preaching companions, Paul knew that if he lost hope in the power of the Spirit and distorted God's word, his ministry would no longer be commendable to God or others (2 Cor. 4:2).[19]

---

visit people in dreams and visions if we were all sharing our testimony faithfully." See Hikmat Kashouh, *Following Jesus in Turbulent Times: Disciple-Making in the Arab World* (Carlisle, UK: Langham, 2018), 17.

18 Allen, *Missionary Methods*, 74.

19 Carson warns that "without the repeated, passionate, Spirit-anointed proclamation of 'Jesus Christ and him crucified,' we may be winning more adherents than converts." Therefore, we

Our Ends Determine Our Means

I once visited an old Armenian Protestant church building in the heart of Istanbul's Golden Horn, only a fifteen-minute walk from the majestic Hagia Sophia. I was there attending meetings with a consortium of Christian ministers from throughout Europe, Asia, and the Middle East. We had converged on this small sanctuary to establish partnerships, collaborate on mission, and formulate new strategies for reaching a specific unreached people group in a nearby region.

Our time together was also an opportunity for encouragement, in part as we heard about those who were laboring in difficult places or on significant projects. In one such case, I was able to attend a breakout session—with no more than seven people in a circle—as we heard a report about a brand-new translation of one of the Gospels. A representative from the translation team was presenting their work, and I was eager to learn about their progress and a potential new resource.

But my enthusiasm quickly turned to dismay.

Since the translation was designed for a particularly challenging audience, the presenter shared how the team had changed their approach. Specifically, instead of retaining the Bible's familial language for God the Father and Son, they were modifying the original wording to be more sensitive to readers from a conservative Muslim background. Recognizing that the Qur'an clearly teaches that Allah has no son (17:111), the translator noted how Muslims flatly reject the notion of Jesus as the Son of God. Others infer from the term "Son" that Christians believe God had sex, presumably

---

should be "fearful of adopting approaches that might empty the cross of Christ of its power" because "the only approval we shall seek is his who tests the quality of each builder's work." See D. A. Carson, *The Cross and Christian Ministry* (Grand Rapids, MI: Baker, 2007), 80–81.

with Mary, resulting in Jesus's birth. This translation would avoid such confusion.[20]

In lieu of "Son," the translators offered a less offensive title, similar to "Authoritative Representative." They felt that by doing so they were being faithful to the original meaning while eliminating a potential stumbling block to Muslims.[21] They were, in a sense, clearing the runway for the gospel to land among this unreached people. In fact, the presenter excitedly reported that initial tests with sample readers produced positive feedback. His whole session was brimming with hope in the possibilities this new translation would create, with the doors it would open.

But the more he basked in their ingenuity, the more I reeled in disbelief, even anger. As he spoke, I could barely contain my frustration. My heart drummed against my chest; my jaw strained. Sitting there in that small group, my mind raced with all I wanted to say—all I felt I had to say. *What of the fact that this is God's unchanging revelation of himself to us? What about the Lord's Prayer? What of Jesus's warnings about being ashamed of the Son?*

Finally, it came to a point where our session opened for discussion. After a bit, I spoke up. But I have no idea what I said. The words came out haltingly. I expressed deep concerns. My voice flared. I pled with them to reconsider. But I couldn't communicate all that I wanted to say. In my mind, this wasn't a legitimate

---

20 Commenting on Paul's flexibility in his missionary approach, David Garland writes: "His accommodation has nothing to do with watering down the gospel message, soft-pedaling its ethical demands, or compromising its absolute monotheism. Paul never modified the message of Christ crucified to make it less of a scandal to Jews or less foolish to Greeks." See David E. Garland, *1 Corinthians* (Grand Rapids, MI: Baker, 2003), 435.

21 See D. A. Carson, *Jesus the Son of God: A Christological Title Often Overlooked, Sometimes Misunderstood, and Currently Disputed* (Wheaton, IL: Crossway, 2012). See also Elliot Clark, "Love Muslims. Proclaim Jesus Is 'Son of God,'" The Gospel Coalition (website), December 10, 2019, https://www.thegospelcoalition.org/.

translation, at least not a faithful one. And even if it managed to bring the blessing of God to more people, I feared it was going to bring the judgment of God upon them.[22]

After a minute or two, someone else in the group asked to speak. He was an Iraqi pastor. As a national leader who had suffered for his faith, he commanded the group's attention. Everyone listened. "You know what you've done, don't you?" he asked in a reprimanding tone. "Every single Muslim believes that our Scriptures are corrupted. In fact, they constantly argue with us and say that the *injil* has been twisted, that we've changed Allah's words." Then he paused, staring straight into the presenter's eyes with clarity and a sure conscience. "Now you've proven them all right," he said. "You *actually have* changed God's word. You know what you've done? You just handed them bullets for their gun."

For a brief moment, the group sat in stunned silence. I assumed his argument landed with force. But I was equally shocked as the presenter casually deflected his comments and, after a short back and forth, doubled down in defense of their translation. The team's intentions were honorable. This resource would reach more people. How could anyone find fault with their work?

To this day, I look back on that experience as one of the most frustrating moments of my life. I was convinced something wrong had happened in that room but felt powerless to do anything about it. I walked out of the church with no clear sense of what to think or how to respond. *Did I overreact? Did I say too much? Or not say enough?* I wasn't sure if I'd spoken out of turn. On the other hand, I wasn't sure if I'd adequately communicated my alarm. But one thing I did know. I'd seen it clearer than ever: in

---

22 Paul the missionary wasn't only concerned for his hearers, but also for himself (1 Cor. 9:23–27).

missions, when reaching others becomes your primary end, you'll easily justify any means.[23]

Innocent of the Blood of All

I can't imagine what someone like Henry Martyn would think of a translation that intentionally removes the identifying title of Jesus as the Son of God. Not just because of developments in translation theory or a desire for contextualized theology. But because missionaries of old were motivated by more than love for the lost and a desire to spread the gospel. Creating a movement of Jesus-followers—to adopt more contemporary terminology—was only one in a multitude of their missionary ambitions.

According to Martyn's biographer, "it was not success that drove him on."[24] Seeing ministry results was subsidiary to a more controlling aspiration. He preached the gospel, seeking to be found faultless. In his personal diary, Martyn regularly reflected on the Lord's commissioning of the prophet Ezekiel to serve as a watchman.

> Son of man, I have made you a watchman for the house of Israel. Whenever you hear a word from my mouth, you shall give them warning from me. If I say to the wicked, "You shall surely die," and you give him no warning, nor speak to warn the wicked from his wicked way, in order to save his life, that wicked person shall die for his iniquity, but his blood I will require at your hand. (Ezek. 3:17–18; cf. 33:7–8)

---

23 I once heard Albert Mohler say that all Christian heresies have their origins in apologetics. Those who set out to defend the faith are often tempted to adjust the gospel to make it more palatable.

24 France, "Henry Martyn," 248.

On the last day, Henry Martyn wanted to be found trustworthy. That was the reason for his commitment to faithfully preserve God's word. That's what turned a timid man into a bold herald. And that same motivation was clearly at the forefront of Paul's thinking throughout his missionary efforts.

We can observe that impulse in his initial entry into Corinth. As Paul begins to preach in the synagogue, and as some of the Jews revile him and rally against his cause, he responds by declaring his innocence of their blood (Acts 18:6).[25] "Innocent," not before Jewish or Greek authorities, but innocent before God. For Paul, the ultimate arbiter of his life and ministry was the Lord himself. And his hope of guiltlessness was based upon his faithful proclamation of God's word as a watchman on the wall.

This is the very inner logic that compelled Paul in Ephesus and elsewhere. As he commends his ministry example to the Ephesian elders at Miletus, Paul testifies that he is "innocent of the blood of all" precisely *because* he "did not shrink from declaring" the complete counsel of God (Acts 20:26–27). He could be sure of his blamelessness before God because he finished the missionary task God gave him. His stewardship was "to testify to the gospel of the grace of God" (Acts 20:24).

We must reckon with this Pauline way of viewing our relationship before God as his ambassadors. If we can conceive of guilt and innocence only in terms of God's objective declaration of our justification in Christ, then we have narrowed the focus of the biblical witness and limited the motivation for missionary faithfulness.

---

25 By declaring his innocence "Paul indicated that he had acted like the faithful watchman in Ezekiel 33:1–9." As such, "he would not be responsible for the punishment of those who rejected the gospel he proclaimed to them." See David G. Peterson, *The Acts of the Apostles* (Grand Rapids, MI: Eerdmans, 2009), 511.

There is a dimension of guilt and innocence that's beyond the initial forgiveness of sins, just as there's an aspect of honor and shame that reaches beyond the resurrection of the body. In Christ, God has dealt decisively with our sin and shame, removing condemnation and guaranteeing glory. But that doesn't mean that we automatically escape the possibility of God finding fault with our labor. That doesn't necessarily free the believer from any possibility of disgrace.

Throughout his ministry, Paul was motivated to preach the gospel by more than just the rearward reference point of the cross and justification. With the day of judgment on the horizon, he was propelled to speak the truth sincerely in pursuit of God's commendation.[26] Therefore, Paul labored that "no fault" be found in his ministry (2 Cor. 6:3; 8:20).[27] Specifically, he emphasized to the Corinthians that he conducted his mission with pure motives and sincere love and by truthful speech (2 Cor. 6:6–7). While they questioned his intentions and treated Paul like an impostor, the apostle's character and integrity demonstrated him to be the genuine article (2 Cor. 6:8). He believed that he was faultless before them because he was innocent before God. In fact, Paul expected to be vindicated before God one day as a direct result of his bold proclamation and blameless reputation.[28]

We Believe, So We Speak

But did Paul preach with boldness and sincerity simply to maintain innocence? Did he proclaim the gospel merely to avoid censure?

---

26 Similarly, Paul's farewell charge to Timothy was to "preach the word" (reprove, rebuke, exhort, and teach) in light of Christ's coming judgment and kingdom (2 Tim. 4:1–2).

27 Paul desired to be above reproach with others (cf. 1 Tim. 3:2; Titus 1:6–7). However, Garland believes that Paul wasn't ultimately concerned that his ministry might be discredited by the Corinthians. "The censure he dreads does not come from humans but from God (1 Cor. 4:1–5)." See Garland, *1 Corinthians*, 306.

28 In Psalm 26, David pleads with God to test, prove, and vindicate him because of his faith that led him to walk in integrity and faithfully proclaim the wondrous deeds of God.

As I have argued in previous chapters, I believe Paul conducted his ministry in order to maximize his reward, boast, and crown of rejoicing on the last day.[29] In the opening of 2 Corinthians, Paul connects his boast with his exemplary character. As he says, "For our boast is this, the testimony of our conscience, that we behaved in the world with simplicity [single-mindedness] and godly sincerity" (2 Cor. 1:12). Paul desires to restore their trust in him such that they will partner with him through prayer "so that many will give thanks on our behalf for the blessing granted us through the prayers of many" (2 Cor. 1:11). Through the help of their prayers—and through his personal integrity—Paul expects the grace of God to reach many, such that they will respond in thanksgiving. Consequently, on the day of Christ many will boast of Paul, as he will of them (2 Cor. 1:14).

Later in the letter, Paul links his ministry team's gospel proclamation with the same goal and a clear vision of the last day. They preach in view of mutual thanksgiving in the presence of Christ. As Paul writes,

> Since we have the same spirit of faith according to what has been written, "I believed, and so I spoke," we also believe, and so we also speak, knowing that he who raised the Lord Jesus will raise us also with Jesus and bring us with you into his presence. For it is all for your sake, so that as grace extends to more and more people it may increase thanksgiving, to the glory of God. (2 Cor. 4:13–15)

In this paragraph Paul quotes from Psalm 116:10. Like the psalmist, his team believes something that leads them to speak

---

29 Proclaiming Christ—warning and teaching everyone—was instrumental to Paul's ability to present his converts as mature in Christ (Col. 1:28).

something.[30] But what do Paul and his fellow workers believe? And what do they speak? In the context, their *speaking* is the proclamation of Jesus Christ as Lord (2 Cor. 4:2, 5). And Paul and his companions are compelled to speak this good news despite much affliction *because* they believe in the resurrection. Just as God raised Jesus, they too will be raised (1 Cor. 15:20). But it's not merely eternal life that motivates their preaching. Paul says they anticipate a resurrection that includes a presentation before God *along with* the Corinthians (2 Cor. 4:14; cf. Jude 24).

Here again, Paul hints at what he stated earlier. He doesn't envision an individualistic reckoning before his Judge. He expects a collective accounting where there will be mutual boasting and shared thanksgiving, all redounding to the glory of God. And that boast and thanksgiving are *increased* as grace extends through Paul's preaching among them and beyond them into new lands. Furthermore, if I'm understanding Paul correctly here, he says this is all *for the Corinthians' sake*. Paul's missionary motivation to faithfully speak the gospel is one of enhancing his own joy, praise, and honor before the Father, as well as that of his ministry partners.

In short, since Paul believes in the possibility of increased rewards and glory, he speaks.[31] Because of the marvelous joy that awaits him, he does not lose heart (2 Cor. 4:1, 16). Therefore, he renounces disgraceful methods and underhanded strategies. He refuses to tamper with God's word. He models reputable business practices and fiscal responsibility. He works hard and sacrifices comforts. He lives in such a way as to commend himself to both God and

30 See the parallels between Paul's situation and the psalmist's in Scott Hafemann, *2 Corinthians: The NIV Application Commentary* (Grand Rapids, MI: Zondervan, 2000), 187.

31 "We conclude that the basis and motive for Paul's 'speaking' are eschatological, specifically in reference to judgment." See Paul Barnett, *The Second Epistle to the Corinthians* (Grand Rapids, MI: Eerdmans, 1997), 243.

others. His statement of the gospel is open, transparent, and bold. Since he believes in a reward, he speaks the truth.

If we are to be missionaries who follow in Paul's footsteps, we must take seriously Paul's example at Corinth and remember his words at Miletus. Every minister of the gospel is called to speak the truth sincerely. We don't do this merely to reach the unreached. We do it because our aim is to please God by faithfully stewarding his gospel. If we fail at that task, it won't matter if we "finish" another one. If we distort God's word or lead others astray, we have no reason to expect his approval. We will not be found innocent.

But if we faithfully carry out our stewardship; if we conduct our business, ministry, and personal ventures with utmost integrity; if we work with single-minded sincerity, living above reproach as an example to the believers; if we faithfully speak the truth to everyone, regardless of the consequences; if we regularly proclaim the gospel and admonish sinners, reasoning from the Scriptures and persuading them of the good news of Jesus—then we can expect an increase to our shared joy and reward. Just as Paul motivated the Ephesian elders, we serve in this way knowing that, as we do, our Lord promises greater blessing.[32]

---

32 Acts 20:35 isn't merely a maxim to counter greed with generosity. Instead, the promise of more blessing is meant to inspire "selfless" sacrifice through a reward in heaven.

6

Setting Boundaries

Macedonia

SALINE TEARS SPILLED down Paul's cheeks, flowing into the creases of his face like a dry riverbed. He wiped them. His calloused hands moistened, softened by sorrow. How could he hope to adequately communicate his love? Though he was wounded by the Corinthians, he harbored no intent to hurt them in return. The anguish and affliction of his heart wasn't overflowing in anger. Paul was writing this letter, painful as it was, with the intent to restore and reconcile.

Following his initial eighteen months in Corinth, Paul had departed eastward along with Aquila and Priscilla. More than a year later, while serving with them in Ephesus, Paul sent Timothy to Corinth carrying the letter we know as 1 Corinthians. At the time, Paul expected to revisit the Achaian believers, spending the winter with them after passing through Macedonia. Then, having gathered a substantial offering for the Jerusalem church, the Corinthians would send him on his way (1 Cor. 16:5–9). But plans change.

Once Timothy returned, Paul learned that all was not well. His lengthy letter—addressing their unhealthy divisions, sexual immorality, and casual attitude toward idolatry—had not been sufficient. Even though ministry opportunities were plentiful in Ephesus, Paul left Asia Minor to make an impromptu visit to Corinth. However, what he intended for good resulted in further harm.

Apparently, someone in the Corinthian congregation challenged the apostle's authority to his face. Along with him, a minority within the church sided against Paul. While most of the body still agreed with him, their support lacked the dynamism to win the day.[1] In the end, Paul departed without the assurance of a committed congregation. His Jerusalem offering appeared in doubt. His Corinthian labors appeared in vain. With their relationship teetering on the brink, Paul forestalled another visit to Achaia and the possibility for further pain (2 Cor. 1:16, 23). Instead, he returned eastward.

It was then that Paul penned his tearful letter to the Corinthians (2 Cor. 2:4). This time, he dispatched Titus to Achaia, still hopeful for a chance at reconciliation. The plan was to reconvene in Troas. But as time ticked away and Titus didn't show, the possible scenarios of further rejection rehearsed themselves in Paul's mind. Fearing the outcome, he set out for Macedonia in hopes of catching Titus there.

When the two finally met in Macedonia, Titus brought a good report. Paul was greatly relieved. Yet there were lingering and significant concerns. False apostles had infiltrated an already divided community. And the ongoing issues of immorality and idolatry still threatened to compromise the church. So from Macedonia,

[1] For background to Paul's painful visit and tearful letter, see Paul Barnett, *The Second Epistle to the Corinthians* (Grand Rapids, MI: Eerdmans, 1997), 28–33.

without delaying any further, Paul started writing what would be his fourth letter to the Corinthians, what we call 2 Corinthians, commending his ministry, appealing for gospel fidelity, encouraging generosity, and warning about false apostles. If Paul was to fulfill his mission, the Corinthians needed to reject the false missionaries among them. They also needed to spurn idolatry and every form of moral impurity. Paul, who had earlier urged for ecclesial unity (1 Cor. 1:10), now pressed for necessary division. Because to be a faithful church involves more than just embracing the gospel and good apostles. You need to set clear boundaries.

Turning from Idols

As a young boy growing up in Scotland, John Gibson Paton was impressed by the prayers of his father during family worship when "he poured out his whole soul with tears" for the heathen world's conversion. "As we rose from our knees," Paton recalled, "I used to look at the light on my father's face, and wish I were like him in spirit." Later in life he remembered that in those early years his desires were awakened to one day become an answer to those prayers. He hoped to serve as a missionary, "privileged and prepared" to take the gospel to the unevangelized.[2]

And Paton did just that. In 1858, John and wife, Mary, reached the remote island of Tanna, on the southern edge of the New Hebrides, now known as Vanuatu, an island country located in the South Pacific Ocean. Upon arrival, Paton mused that if anywhere in the world a people might be atheistic—without a custom of religion or a worship of idols—it would surely be the isolated and virgin island

2 John G. Paton, *John G. Paton: Missionary to the New Hebrides*, ed. by James Paton (Edinburgh: Banner of Truth, 2007), 21.

of Tanna. Yet he found the New Hebrides to be a nation where the locals, "destitute of the knowledge of the true God, are ceaselessly groping after Him." However, since they had not found him, "not being able to live without some sort of God," Paton wrote, "they have made idols of almost everything."[3]

Reminiscent of Paul in Greece, Paton walked into a world full of deities and took the opportunity to make known the unknown God. In doing so, he also made it clear that any who would follow in the way of Jesus must turn away from their previous worship. Their former idolatry was no longer an option. But as Paton began to teach the nationals that to worship and serve God "they must cast aside all their idols and leave off every heathen custom and vice, they rose in anger and cruelty" toward the missionary—going so far as to persecute anyone who was welcoming of his foreign mission.[4]

Paul's experience was much the same. Despite the apostle's ability to connect with his Greek counterparts about their pursuit of knowledge and impulse to worship (Acts 17:22–23), his message consistently called on sinners to turn from idols to serve the living God (1 Thess. 1:9).[5] While Paul was willing to be like the Greeks to win the Greek, his accommodation had limits. His gospel was not simply the opportunity to add another immortal to the pantheon of worship. Paul's preaching tore down the religious system of his converts' former ignorance (Acts 17:30; Eph. 4:18). As Jesus promised, Paul's gospel wielded a sword—dividing people from their former religion, their previous way of life, and sometimes unavoidably separating friends and families (Matt. 10:34).

3 Paton, *John G. Paton*, 73.
4 Paton, *John G. Paton*, 74.
5 "Paul's call to turn from idols was fundamental to his proclamation of the gospel (1 Thess. 1:9; cf. Acts 14:15; Rom. 1:22–25; 1 Cor. 5:10, 11; 6:9)." See Barnett, *The Second Epistle to the Corinthians*, 350.

The problem in Achaia was that some of the believers didn't understand this. They had yet to make a clean break from idolatry. In the Corinthian correspondence, we see Paul take pains to point out the error of false worship among them. Perhaps some thought their participation in pagan rituals was inconsequential since idols are, in fact, nonexistent (1 Cor. 8:4). But while they had adopted a dismissive demeanor toward various activities, Paul urges for separation, exhorting them to flee idolatry (1 Cor. 10:14). Even though the apostle will happily acknowledge that an idol is nothing more than wood, stone, or metal, he understands that behind them stand principalities and powers (1 Cor. 10:19–20; cf. Deut. 32:16–17). To participate in the sacrifice of food offered to idols isn't merely a matter of conscience or Christian consideration for the "weaker brother." The act itself has the potential to be personally damaging.[6] Pagan worship isn't a neutral activity, an option of Christian liberty, which some might choose to continue for the sake of maintaining familial or social harmony. According to Paul, "You cannot partake of the table of the Lord and the table of demons" (1 Cor. 10:21; cf. Isa. 65:11).

Reaching back before the letter of 1 Corinthians and stretching up to Paul's final visit, this topic is clearly one of ongoing concern. For all the issues that make up the Corinthian problem, idolatry is the consistent issue that Paul feels compelled to address.[7] In 2 Corinthians, he returns to the topic once again, restating the need for the church's wholesale separation from idolatry in a flourish of

---

6 Partaking of the table of the Lord in an unworthy manner can also bring judgment (1 Cor. 11:29).

7 Barnett's view is that ongoing Corinthian participation in Greco-Roman pagan worship and idolatry was "the circumstance that precipitated his emergency visit and the writing of the 'Severe Letter.'" See Barnett, *The Second Epistle to the Corinthians*, 343.

Old Testament citations that demand purity for the people of God (2 Cor. 6:16–18; cf. 1 Cor. 10:1–11).

As we've seen thus far, Paul unrolls the parchment of 2 Corinthians to defend his apostolic authority and commend his new covenant ministry. But to what end? Is Paul egocentric, self-conscious, or soft, unable to handle rejection from others? No, Paul isn't so much concerned for his reputation as he is the Corinthians' preservation. His goal of proving his love and regaining their trust serves the greater goal of securing their faith. He wants them to bring "holiness to completion" (2 Cor. 7:1). That's why Paul spends the first six chapters laying bare his heart before the Achaian believers. He asks them to enlarge their hearts to him—and to the commands of God—resulting in their separation from idolatry (2 Cor. 6:11–13; cf. Ps. 119:32).

The climax of Paul's apologia for his apostolate—the centerpiece of 2 Corinthians—is his plea for them to separate from the temple cults of Corinth.[8] His persuasive rhetoric and the repeated aims at commending his ministry crescendo in this one command: "Do not be unequally yoked with unbelievers" (2 Cor. 6:14). By this curious metaphor of a mixed team of animals, Paul clearly has in mind something more than mixed marriage, and something other than total separation from the world.[9] His specific concern is more focused. He wants the Corinthians to separate from lawlessness, darkness, and Belial. The believer's share is not with an idola-

---

8   I'm borrowing language here from Barnett, *The Second Epistle to the Corinthians*, 341. Garland believes Paul is primarily concerned with eating meat offered to idols, which he associates with idolatry, "even if the Christian eating this food has no intention of bowing down to serve idols." See David E. Garland, *2 Corinthians* (Nashville: B&H, 1999), 333.

9   A survey of the Corinthian correspondence reveals that Paul doesn't call for wholesale separation from the world (1 Cor. 5:9–10; 7:12–16, 39; 8:10; 9:21; 10:27, 32; 14:23). See the helpful and concise summary in C. K. Barrett, *The Second Epistle to the Corinthians* (London: A & C Black, 1986), 196.

trous unbeliever. The temple of God—that is, God's new covenant people—must have nothing to do with idols (2 Cor. 6:14–16; cf. Num. 25:1–3; Ps. 106:28).

Temple of God

I remember the first time I visited Nepal and strolled among Kathmandu's Hindu temples, stupas, and seemingly endless *murti*. I vividly recall standing on a hill overlooking Pashupatinath Temple and observing with grief the irony of an enormous statue of a golden cow. I remember pushing down nausea as the smoke from burning bodies rose from the Bagmati River below. I also recall sitting every morning in the courtyard of my hotel, waiting for breakfast as the server offered a sacrifice to a motionless god. It all made me ill. In a mixture of sorrow, sickness, and frustration, my spirit was provoked within me (Acts 17:16).

Those words are perhaps offensive to some. But whereas the best Christian preaching is sympathetic, compassionate, and reconciliatory, it is also exclusivist. We do not claim to have a positive view of world religions, despite all the positive actions and noble beliefs of their adherents. Historically, Christians have held that all other religions are fundamentally opposed to the Christian gospel and are principally in error. While their teachings contain truths, they are not ultimately true, nor are they from God. While their worship acknowledges some deity—even a creator—it is idolatrous.[10] While those of other religions might visit a holy place or solemn temple, they are not of the true temple, the one people of God.

---

10 Daniel Strange argues extensively that the nature of non-Christian religion and religions is fundamentally idolatrous. See Daniel Strange, *Their Rock Is Not Like Our Rock: A Theology of Religions* (Grand Rapids, MI: Zondervan, 2014).

However, according to the Bible, believers in Jesus from every nation who turn to God from idols join that one people, enter Christ's kingdom, and become stones in God's temple (1 Pet. 2:4–10). This was the significant conclusion of the Jerusalem Council. Gentiles in Asia who were partakers of the Spirit through Paul's missionary endeavors were counted as fulfilling the Old Testament prophecy about the rebuilding of David's tent (Acts 15:16; cf. Amos 9:11).[11] They were the true tabernacle, the temple of God, with God's presence dwelling among them. As such, they need not be circumcised. They were no longer considered unclean. However—and this is crucial—they did need "to abstain from the things polluted by idols, and from sexual immorality, and from what has been strangled, and from blood" (Acts 15:20; cf. Lev. 17–18).

I do not believe these instructions from the Jerusalem Council were imposing Mosaic standards, simply encouraging "table fellowship" between Gentiles and Jews, or requesting Gentile believers to make concessions for the sake of their "weak" Jewish brothers and sisters. Instead, the Council recognized the connection between these prohibitions and idolatrous Gentile practices of the time. For them, pursuing the worship of God required severing ties with idolatry.[12]

More than a century ago, Roland Allen lamented that this perspective toward false religions had diminished as Western missionaries were rethinking their primary task. Christian preachers were calling Hindu individuals to faith in Jesus without expecting the

---

11 See G. K. Beale, *The Temple and the Church's Mission: A Biblical Theology of the Dwelling Place of God* (Downers Grove, IL: IVP, 2004), 232–37.

12 For an argument that the four prohibitions from Acts 15 address idol worship, see Beale, *Temple*, 239–41. See also Doug Coleman, "The Jerusalem Council and the Insider Movement Paradigm," *Global Missiology* 1, no. 12 (October 2014), http://www.global missiology.org/.

kind of exclusion that often follows baptism and the renunciation of caste. Rather than "call men from the heathen temple into the Church of God," Allen noted, some missionaries were seeking to "trim the dimly glowing lamp of God in the heathen temple, and to pour into it a few drops of the oil of Christian doctrine till it shines with a new radiance."[13]

This, he argued, distorted the Pauline approach. While the apostle affirms that the only condition to new life in Christ is faith, such faith involves and assumes a necessary break with all other faiths. The worship of the true God coincides with renouncing all other gods. As Allen reflected on Paul's missionary method, he emphasized the necessary division that Paul's apostolic preaching requires:

> He did not preach that the mission of the Gospel was to reveal the true beauty of heathen religions; but that it was to open a door of salvation to those who would flee from the wrath to come. . . . He did not minimize the breach between Christianity and heathenism; he declared that the one was the kingdom of evil, the other the Kingdom of God, and that his work was to turn men "from darkness to light and from the power of Satan unto God."[14]

For Paul and the apostles, turning to God and to his kingdom was one and the same with becoming the temple of God. But to be God's temple implies isolation from other forms of (Satanic) worship and inclusion into the broader people of God. When Paul makes moral demands on the Corinthian congregation, he

---

13 Roland Allen, *Missionary Methods: St. Paul's or Ours?* (Grand Rapids, MI: Eerdmans, 1962), 70–71.
14 Allen, *Missionary Methods*, 72–73.

can appeal to an individual's status as the temple of God (1 Cor. 6:19), but he can also emphasize their corporate responsibility. As the eschatological temple, they should conform to a collective standard and custom among other churches (1 Cor. 7:17; 11:16; cf. 1 Thess. 2:14). If James and the Jerusalem Council advise against ongoing participation in idolatrous practice, Paul would expect all churches to abide by their decision.

Therefore, when Paul writes to the Corinthians, he repeatedly reminds them how their new identity as the temple of God should separate them from idolatry. They must no longer associate with the worship of pagan temples.[15] Since God has made his dwelling among them, they are called to go out from among their idolatrous neighbors. They should, in keeping with Isaiah's warning, "touch no unclean thing" (Isa. 52:11). Only then, Paul reasons, can they be confident of the Lord's welcome, as he becomes for them a Father, making the Corinthians his sons and daughters (2 Cor. 6:16–18).

Paul's warning is stark. The dividing wall between Jew and Gentile is demolished (Eph. 2:14), but there yet remains a distinct boundary around God's holy temple.[16] Therefore, he implores the Corinthians to cleanse themselves from every defilement in the fear of the Lord (2 Cor. 7:1). But here again the apostle is their prototype. Paul only expects what he also exemplifies. As he has already told the Corinthians, Paul conducts all his ministry in the fear of

---

15 "Just as it was inconceivable that idols could be brought into the temple of Yahweh, so under the new dispensation it is impossible for the temple of God, the members of the holy congregation of God (1 Cor. 1:2), to go to or share in the cultic worship of idols in Gentile Corinth (1 Cor. 10:14–22; cf. 8:10–13)." See Barnett, *The Second Epistle to the Corinthians*, 349–50.

16 Paul doesn't expect social separation from idolaters (1 Cor. 5:9–10). The distinct boundary he sets is directly related to participation in idolatrous worship practices. However, discernment is required when the line is blurry between what is cultural and what constitutes false worship.

the Lord, knowing that he will one day give an account before his Judge. This is why he takes care how he, as a missionary, lays the stones and forms the structure of the temple of God. Those who build well will receive a reward, while those who build poorly will suffer loss (1 Cor. 3:14–15). However, there is another possible outcome for the builders of God's people: "If anyone destroys God's temple, God will destroy him" (1 Cor. 3:17; cf. Matt. 18:6).

Separating from False Missionaries

As someone who grew up in the home of a pastor, I've been around churches and missionaries for my entire life. Having served as a supported worker for over a decade, I've also had the privilege of visiting scores of churches, speaking with elder boards and mission committees across the country. Now that I'm part of a ministry that teaches church leaders around the world, I've also had the opportunity to meet with and serve alongside residential missionaries on multiple continents. And while many of the missionaries I know are doing wonderful work, there are inevitable exceptions.

This shouldn't be a shock to us. False teachers and false teaching aren't an "out there" problem. As the Ephesian elders needed to recognize, false teachers *will* spring up like weeds in our own garden (Acts 20:29–30). I don't think this means that every church invariably has a wolf among the sheep or that every mission agency is corrupted by false missionaries. But it does mean that we need to be sober and on alert. If elders in a local church are prone to wander, then surely isolated and far-flung missionaries are in danger when surrounded by adherents to other religions. Having lived for a time as an extreme minority, one of ten believers in a city of half a million, I know it's not easy. I've felt the doubts creeping in. The exclusive claims of Christ have weighed heavily upon me. I've *wanted* to be wrong. And I know missionaries in similar situations who decided they were.

What's particularly troubling to me is that wherever I travel in the United States, I find churches unaware of what their supported and sent-out workers believe. Elders and committees are disconnected from the field, often telling me that they haven't heard from some missionaries in many months. At times, they admit that they don't even know who they are—having been vetted by others and grandfathered into a system of guaranteed monthly support. Not surprisingly, then, these churches don't know what their missionaries actually believe or practice, much less how to hold them accountable.

Furthermore, most churches and pastors are largely uninformed about missiological trends, discussions, and methods on the field. One growing concern of mine is to equip churches to be aware of what missionaries are doing and what many organizations are encouraging. Whenever I share some of my observations and experiences from overseas, many pastors and church leaders are either stunned or appalled. They're also overwhelmed, not knowing how to respond.

I believe an appropriate response starts with awareness and clear communication. Churches—and even individual donors[17]—need to talk with their supported workers about their theological vision and methodological approach. It's not enough for missionaries to say that they want to start a church or make disciples. It's not enough for churches to ask about results—who has been reached or how many groups are gathering. The questions need to go deeper. And before entering the discussion, churches need to know what they value, what they believe, and how they will respond.

---

17 Individuals could benefit from seeking the wisdom of their churches in making support decisions.

While I'm certainly not advocating for a medieval inquisition on supported workers, simply focusing on education and awareness will not be enough. The Bible is clear that Christians and churches must not send and fund those who are leading others astray (2 John 10; cf. 1 John 4:1). Sometimes information gathering will necessarily lead to establishing better boundaries. But potentially it will end in ministry separation—which leads us to Paul's second action point in 2 Corinthians.

Not only does Paul expect the Achaian believers to turn away from idolatry and immorality, he also intends for them to reject and defund the false missionaries who had infiltrated their community. In our English translations—and depending on one's understanding of the word *apostle*—it's easy to overlook the simple fact that when Paul calls out the false apostles in Corinth, he's identifying false *missionaries*. He calls them "deceitful workmen," those who are boasting in their misguided "mission" (2 Cor. 11:12–13). As it turns out, Paul isn't the only missionary in town. And he isn't afraid to label others as fraudulent and false. Because, in his understanding, they aren't true missionaries of Christ. They're servants of Satan.

This is striking for at least two reasons. First, if the false apostles in Corinth were interviewed by the average missions committee, they would no doubt identify themselves as servants of Christ. Commentators understand that Paul is, in his stinging rebuke, using their own language against them.[18] They think themselves to be on the side of right, messengers of light, holding forth the word of Christ. But Paul sees them differently. They are deceitful and disguised, misleading the Corinthians and likely deceiving their

---

18 See Barnett, *The Second Epistle to the Corinthians*, 35–36. See also Philip Hughes, *Paul's Second Epistle to the Corinthians* (Grand Rapids, MI: Eerdmans, 1962), 394–96.

own selves. This brings us to the second surprising aspect in Paul's evaluation of their ministry. He describes their work with the same terms and imagery that he earlier used to illustrate idolatry. This literary feature reveals that, in Paul's mind, the false missionaries at Corinth are no different from the pagan gods of Greece. They are leading others into darkness, wickedness, and the realm of Satan.[19] They are guilty of destroying the temple of God. As such, "their end will correspond to their deeds" (2 Cor. 11:15).

If Paul's climactic paraenesis in 2 Corinthians aims at unburdening the Corinthians from a yoke of idolatry, he has similar ambitions for their mismatched relationship with misleading teachers. He wants the church to not be unequally yoked with false missionaries.[20] In both cases, the believers in Achaia need to learn discernment. They need to set clear boundaries. That includes relinquishing their former idolatrous practice. By implication, it also means rescinding their support for spurious missionaries and false teachers.

Abstaining from Foods Sacrificed

I remember the first time I had a tinge of concern about questionable missionary practice. I was visiting a Muslim country, and my host shared a story of how their team was trying to adapt to the culture and reach the community. This led them to offer their own sacrificial lamb during the Muslim holiday of sacrifice. They did so to show solidarity with their neighbors, participate in the local customs, and demonstrate their Christian piety. Like many of the

---

19 Conversely, Paul's mission was to deliver people from darkness and Satan (Acts 26:18).

20 Elsewhere Paul can employ similar imagery ("yokefellow") to describe a ministry partner (Phil. 4:3). The early church, at the Council of Sardica, also applied the command to not be unequally yoked specifically to the issue of separation from false teachers. See Hughes, *The Second Epistle to the Corinthians*, 250–51.

Muslims around them, they took the slaughtered animal and gave some of its meat to the poor.

According to the teaching of Islam, those submitted to Allah cut the yearly sacrifice in remembrance of Abraham's willingness to sacrifice his son, Ishmael, and as a way to share with others. The local tradition in that part of the world was to keep a third of the meat for one's family, share a third with friends or extended family, and give a third to the poor. Like so many other Islamic traditions, their religious practice demonstrates genuine hospitality and generosity.

When our family later moved to that same region, friends and neighbors would show up at our door during the yearly sacrifice with warm, red meat in a plastic grocery bag dripping with blood. Despite the awkward method of delivery, we appreciated their kindness and accepted the offering. After all, meat from the market was quite expensive, and we didn't want to offend our neighbors. However, I always had a nagging thought in the back of my mind. *Should we really accept this?*

As time went on, our family developed relationships with local believers and became more involved with a local church. Out of curiosity, we began to ask what they did over the Muslim holiday of sacrifice. Without fail, all our national friends from multiple churches revealed that they would always refuse the meat.[21] Not that they were indignant or rude about it. But they would graciously tell others that they believed the death of Jesus on the cross represented the final sacrifice. They couldn't accept meat that had been offered to Allah.

---

21 Early Christian communities were reviled throughout the Roman Empire for their "obstinacy," for refusing to participate in common practices such as offering "a pinch of incense on a pagan altar." See Christopher A. Hall, *Living Wisely with the Church Fathers* (Downers Grove, IL: IVP, 2017), 36–39.

Needless to say, as I became aware of their consensus, I was increasingly concerned about the common practice among missionaries to receive meat from our Muslim neighbors. First of all, I didn't want to go against what seemed to be the custom of local churches. Nevertheless, I still wanted to be involved, as much as possible, in the local community and culture. I wasn't sure if this was an issue of biblical conviction or perhaps a personal preference that would unnecessarily erect barriers to evangelistic engagement. I wanted to be "all things to all people."

But as I considered the witness of the New Testament generally,[22] and as I focused on Paul's argument in 1 Corinthians specifically, I became increasingly concerned that many in the missions community were too easily dismissive of the dangers associated with idol meat. For example, while Paul does make concessions regarding the nature of meat offered to idols, his instruction doesn't end there. It's important to see that 1 Corinthians 8–10 represents a single, progressing unit of thought.[23] Whereas Paul begins by urging the Corinthians to relinquish their right to eat for the sake of weak brothers and sisters, he ultimately transitions to address the inherent risks for the supposedly strong.[24]

"Therefore," Paul urges, "let anyone who thinks that he stands take heed lest he fall" (1 Cor. 10:12). Those who casually participate in pagan rituals or sacrifices are warned that they—not just weaker Christians—might be tempted beyond what they're able to

---

22 Acts 15:20, 29; 21:25; 1 Cor. 8:10; 10:21; 2 Cor. 6:16; 1 John 5:21; Rev. 2:14, 20.

23 See Alex T. Cheung, *Idol Food in Corinth: Jewish Background and Pauline Legacy* (Sheffield, England: Sheffield Academic, 1999), 115–17.

24 While there is significant overlap between the concerns for weaker Christians in 1 Cor. 8:1–11:1 and Romans 14:1–15:13, the issues addressed are distinct. Schreiner believes Paul does not permit the knowing consumption of idol meat, equating it with idolatry. See Thomas R. Schreiner, *1 Corinthians: An Introduction and Commentary* (Downers Grove, IL: IVP, 2018), 162–66.

withstand (cf. 1 Cor. 10:13). Paul is concerned they may succumb, like the Israelites of old, to the allure of false worship. Therefore, he offers God's way of escape: they should "flee idolatry" (1 Cor. 10:14).[25] Even though an idol isn't really anything, Paul won't provoke the Lord to jealousy by taking the cup of the Lord and the cup of demons (1 Cor. 10:19–22). In the apostle's opinion, you cannot gather with the Lord's people on the Lord's day and take from the Lord's Table while still partaking in pagan food rites at the temple down the road.

However, I still wasn't totally clear how our situation mirrored Paul's. My missionary colleagues (or, for that matter, my Muslim friends) weren't offering animals to graven images. Nor were they eating sacrificed meat within a temple. Perhaps, some might argue, they weren't even participating in an expressly religious ritual. And even if their sacrifice was offered in submission to Allah, it wasn't to any random deity but to, in their minds, the God of Abraham and the Creator of all.

Despite the many complicating factors, our family concluded that we shouldn't accept the meat from our Muslim neighbors, in no small measure due to the perspective of local believers. And we certainly wouldn't offer our own Christianized sacrifice on a Muslim holiday. Instead, we felt compelled by the same reasoning that I find in John Paton's own experience on the island of Tanna, when the nationals there offered him a feast following their ceremonial worship. As Paton explained,

Their insisting upon me taking their present of food, laid upon me an unpleasant and dangerous necessity of explaining my

---

25 "Everything in the argument from chapter 8 on has been building to this admonition. Eating in the temple of idols is nothing less than idolatry." See Schreiner, *1 Corinthians*, 209.

refusal. I again thanked them very warmly, and explained that, as they had in my presence given away all their food to an Idol-God and asked his blessing on it as a sacrifice . . . my people and I durst not and could not eat of it, for that would be to have fellowship with their Idols and to dishonor Jehovah God.[26]

For Paton, when offered idol meat, it didn't matter that he wasn't dining in a physical temple. It didn't matter whether or not he was, in his heart, worshiping the true God. It also didn't ultimately matter if his decision would offend others, or worse, invite persecution. Instead, Paton refused, compelled by the logic of Paul. To have fellowship with their idols would be to break fellowship with his God.

Danger from Within

Paton's experience and my own are only a small illustration of a much broader conversation within the evangelical missions community about the degree to which a Christian is able to participate in the customs, forms, and rituals of another religion. The issue isn't a question about whether new followers of Jesus can maintain relationships with unbelievers and remain within their cultures and communities. That much is assumed. Instead, missionaries are asking whether it's allowable, if not desirable, for followers of Jesus to remain engaged within existing socioreligious structures in an effort to influence family and friends in a culturally integrated movement of the gospel.

The impetus for these considerations is typically a good one. Missionaries want to eliminate stumbling blocks to the gospel and reach as many people as possible. Like Paul, they want to adapt

---

26 Paton, *John G. Paton*, 134.

in diverse situations, becoming like people in order to love people (1 Cor. 9:19–23). They also want new believers to reach out to their nearest relations. Sadly, new converts to Christianity are sometimes quick to disassociate from their former communities and even their families, distancing themselves from the very people they're best positioned to reach. In contexts that are hostile to the gospel, perhaps they separate out of shame or for personal security. But whatever the impulse, the result is that some new believers limit their own opportunities for witness and stunt the potential spread of the gospel among indigenous groups.

In response to this challenge, many missionaries now advocate for Insider Movements (IMs).[27] While these movements can encompass a broad range of beliefs and practices, Rebecca Lewis, herself a proponent of IMs, concisely defines them as "movements to obedient faith in Christ that remain integrated with or *inside* their natural community."[28] Such an approach sounds commendable. But in addition to that otherwise benign definition, Lewis adds two important distinctives of these movements. First, believers "are not gathered from diverse social networks to create a 'church.' New parallel social structures are not invented or introduced."[29] Second, new believers are encouraged to "*retain their identity* as members of their socio-religious community."[30]

---

27 For some examples, see Harley Talman and John Jay Travis, eds., *Understanding Insider Movements: Disciples of Jesus within Diverse Religious Communities* (Pasadena, CA: William Carey Library, 2015).

28 Rebecca Lewis, "Insider Movements: Honoring God-Given Identity and Community," *International Journal of Frontier Missiology* 26, no. 1 (Spring 2009): 16.

29 This conflicts with the basic definition of a church (*ekklesia*) as a distinct gathering of believers. Furthermore, Paul's witness to the collective practice of "all the churches" suggests a level of catholicity to the faith based on the apostolic witness (2 Thess. 2:15; 2 Tim. 1:14). Indigenous theologies and individual practices should not divert from this.

30 Lewis, "Insider Movements," 16.

Practically, these characteristics can manifest in a variety of ways. In the case of those coming to Christ in a Hindu context, they might be encouraged to worship Jesus in their temple of preference, apart from or in addition to a separate Christian gathering. Meanwhile, a Buddhist who trusts in Jesus could be encouraged to continue participating in traditions associated with ancestral worship so as not to estrange family or dishonor them. Typically, followers of Jesus coming from an Islamic background may be encouraged to continue attending the mosque and remain a Muslim, perhaps describing themselves as "Muslims in the way of Isa." In some versions of IMs, Mohammed is still accepted as a prophet and the Qur'an as containing divine revelation.[31] In every situation, the goal is to reach those *within* the new believer's preexisting community of religious practice by remaining *within* the socioreligious spheres of influence to create a positive movement of others to faith in Jesus.

Over the last year, I've had the opportunity to talk with missionaries from Europe, Central Asia, North Africa, the Middle East, and South Asia, all working in Muslim contexts. Some of them live in extremely difficult locations. But they were all deeply concerned by those in their regions or countries of service who are proponents of IMs. In fact, some of these IM advocates serve with the same agency or are supported by the same church. Yet when I talk with supporting churches about IMs, I rarely find pastors who are aware of IMs, much less whether their sent-out missionaries are approving of them.

This is of grave concern to me. For all the gray areas of Christian liberty in a colorful world of cultural diversity, I'm convinced that

---

31 For more examples and an assessment of these movements, see Ayman S. Ibrahim and Ant Greenham, eds. *Muslim Conversions to Christ: A Critique of Insider Movements in Islamic Contexts* (New York: Peter Lang, 2018).

many Insider Movements are in direct conflict with the gospel of Jesus Christ and the teaching of the apostles. I am also convinced that if Paul the missionary were living today, he would respond to this as he did to the Corinthians long ago. He would call out the worship of anyone or anything other than the Christ of Scripture to be idolatrous and demonic. He would warn us to flee idolatry. He would plead with us to not be self-confident in our standing, but to watch out for our own falling.

Doug Coleman is a missionary who has extensively analyzed and written about Insider Movements.[32] He believes, as do I, that 1 Corinthians 8–10 is a key passage for considering the biblical warrant for participation in any kind of non-Christian religious ritual. Based on Paul's instructions to the Corinthians, Coleman argues that Christians cannot participate in rites from other religions "regardless of motivation and in spite of attempts at reinterpretation."[33] In other words, attending Friday prayers and prostrating toward Mecca is forbidden for the believer in Jesus, even if that prayer is inwardly directed toward the Lord. Similarly, placing flowers before a graven image in a Hindu ceremony is prohibited, even if the offering of the heart is Godward.[34]

32 Doug Coleman, *A Theological Analysis of the Insider Movement Paradigm from Four Perspectives: Theology of Religions, Revelation, Soteriology and Ecclesiology* (Pasadena, CA: WCIU Press, 2011).

33 Doug Coleman, "The Idol's Temple and the Insider Movement Paradigm: An Examination of 1 Corinthians 8–10," *Global Missiology* 3, no. 12 (April 2015), http://www.globalmissiology.org/. One's understanding of anthropology and the sacraments inevitably contributes to this discussion. In my view, Paul teaches that the Lord's Table involves real participation in the sacrifice and the spiritual presence of Christ (1 Cor. 10:16). Similarly, eating meat as part of a ritual in an idol temple involves real participation in the sacrifice and with the demonic. At issue with Paul is the physical, embodied act within certain rituals or forms, not merely the intent of the worshiper's heart.

34 Origen understands that God forbids both worshiping other gods and bowing before them (Exod. 20:5), warning "a man inclined to idolatry not to practise it." Drawing from

While we might get hung up on the differences between various forms, settings, and objects of worship, Coleman insists that "the more important question is whether a fundamental similarity connects" the situation in Corinth with any of our current settings. In other words, it matters not whether animal sacrifice is directly involved, or even a religious feast at a pagan temple.[35] "The bigger problem," he suggests, "is the fact that somehow participation in a pagan religious ritual amounts to 'titular idolatry.'" And "as long as the particular religious expression or interpretation of any religion is idolatrous, participation in that religion's *religious* rituals is prohibited for the follower of Jesus."[36]

I believe that the Old Testament examples Paul cites in 1 Corinthians 10 add further depth to this discussion. Israel fell into idolatry when they "sat down to eat and drink and rose up to play" (1 Cor. 10:7; cf. Ex. 32:6). This quotation comes from the story at Sinai, when Aaron formed the golden calf and called the children of Israel to worship. When they bowed down before the idol, making sacrifices to it, in their hearts they were inaugurating a feast to the Lord (Ex. 32:4–5). In other words, the Israelite descent into idolatry began with combining the worship of the true God with the pagan rites of the nations.

And what was the result? Even though Israel had been redeemed from slavery and were "baptized," even though they ate manna

---

Num. 25:1–5, he argues that the physical act of bowing before a god (even when feigning worship) is itself a serious sin. Origen, *Prayer*, 146. Interestingly, God was angry when the people of Israel ate food sacrificed to idols and bowed down to them, an event described as Israel "yoking" himself to Baal of Peor (Num. 25:3).

35 An example of this could be visiting the asclepion (healing temples) of Corinth and ancient Greece where devotees would drink from a spring and lie among serpents to receive healing. Paul notably refers to drinking and serpents in his warning against idolatry (1 Cor. 10:4, 9). (A missionary colleague in Greece pointed this out to me.)

36 Coleman, "Idol's Temple."

and drank from the Rock, they were overthrown in the wilderness like Pharaoh in the sea. This was owing to their shared idolatry (1 Cor. 10:1–5).

From Paul's perspective, the Corinthians' experience is running on parallel tracks. They too have been called out and baptized. They too partake of spiritual food and drink when they come to the Lord's Table. But if they continue in idolatrous practices, they're heading to the same dead end as the wilderness generation. Like Israel, they're in danger of being overthrown. Therefore, Paul wants the Corinthians to sober up to the peril of idolatry. Their slip won't likely start with the wholehearted worship of Aphrodite or Poseidon. But it might begin with casually eating meals in an idol temple. If they continue down the same path, Paul says, they're tempting the judgment of God.

But not just the Corinthians. The same is true for those who wield the chisel and carry the hammer in the service of God's house. These ministers seek to build on the solid foundation of Christ, yet they may, in the process, be destroying the very temple of God.

If my analysis is correct, then some missionaries are tempting God's judgment by virtue of their very strategies to advance the gospel. I realize that is a weighty claim. I don't make it lightly, recklessly, or with impunity. But I believe with all my heart that the actions of some missionaries constitute a grievous error by unintentionally promoting idolatry, with potentially terrifying results. By saying that, I do not question their ministry's intent. But I ask them to question its likely end. I simply don't know how else to understand Paul's severe warnings to the Corinthians and his sober words to all Christian ministers. As such, I can't help but pen these words in fear. I do so with tears.

Plea for Discernment

As I write this chapter, the Church of Holy Wisdom, the great Hagia Sophia in Istanbul—one of the oldest and largest cathedrals in the world—has just been turned from a museum into a mosque. In response, leaders from around the world, including those from the United Nations, have voiced their concern, regret, and even outrage to the nation of Turkey. The cultural and religious heritage of that brick-and-mortar structure, they argue, is now endangered.

But if secular society is so concerned by the cultural damage done through converting a historic structure into a holy space for Islamic worship, if they see this as an atrocity—to transform a Christian building into a Muslim house of prayer—and if they recognize it as socially offensive and religiously inappropriate, how is it that Christian missionaries don't see it as even more so to encourage believers in Jesus Christ—the true temple of God—to worship in Hindu temples and Islamic mosques, among worthless idols and countless demons? How do we not see this as an unequal yoke, unfitting of any follower of Christ?

To borrow Paul's line of reasoning, what fellowship does Jesus have with Buddha? What agreement does the light of the gospel have with the darkness of Satan? What communion does the temple of God have with the temple of Shiva? What partnership does the Bible have with the Qur'an?

This chapter is my plea to the church for discernment—to recover our own holy wisdom. Our mission isn't simply to send and support whomever will go to the nations in the name of Jesus. Churches are responsible for their missionaries; therefore, they must be careful whom they commission and commend. They must set and stand by gospel boundaries.[37] Not everyone who goes into all the world is good (1 John 4:1). Not everyone who asks for support is worthy of it (2 John 10). It falls to the church to discerningly partner with missionaries for the sake of the gospel. We should approve only what is excellent (Phil 1:3–10).

But this chapter is also my plea to missionaries. Brothers and sisters, we will give an account one day for our work. As Jesus taught, we could do many great deeds in his name yet have our labors deemed lawless (Matt. 7:21–23). We could zealously cross land and sea for God's sake only to make converts to the wrong cause, a child of hell rather than a child of heaven (Matt. 23:15). We could give our lives to build on the cornerstone of Christ, yet in the end have that stone fall on us (1 Cor. 3:10–17).[38] When we stand before the throne one day, it's possible not just to miss out on reward and commendation. It's possible to face condemnation.

This awareness was at the forefront of Paul's mind as he went about his earthly ministry, and even as he warned the Corinthians of their own peril. Although Paul's ambition was to win as many people as possible, and even though he was willing to make concessions and relinquish his rights to do so, he also made sure he didn't slip up along the way. Since he desired the Father's approval, he disciplined himself as he ran the race. He recognized the route markers. He stayed within his lane. Paul didn't want to come to the finish line and be disqualified.[39]

---

37 See Gavin Ortlund, *Finding the Right Hills to Die On: The Case for Theological Triage* (Wheaton, IL: Crossway, 2020), 76–80.

38 See Barrett, *The Second Epistle to the Corinthians*, 287.

39 In 1 Cor. 9:24–27, Paul transitions from instruction about giving up one's rights to warning against idolatry. Like the apostle, the Corinthians should practice self-discipline for the sake of self-preservation.

Likewise, Jesus doesn't want us to be disqualified. The purpose of God's warnings, and the intent of this chapter, is that we all, churches and missionaries alike, might experience the joy and reward of God's commendation. The Lord provides us with a rule, not so we'll stumble and fail to reach the goal, but so we'll attain glory and honor and immortality. Our Lord is waiting at the podium, and he desires to crown us in praise. But like any race, the potential for a prize doesn't simply propel us to run with pace. It compels us to mind the boundary lines.

7

Sacrificing Like the Savior

Jerusalem

HE HAD BEEN WARNED not to go. Imprisonment—if not worse—
awaited the apostle. But much like his Savior, Paul set his face
toward Jerusalem. Like a lamb to the slaughter, he went willingly.
To the holy mountain, the temple of God, and the place of sacrifice.
He was marching to Zion, returning from the coastlands to present
a priestly offering of the Gentiles.[1]

Weeks earlier, Paul had departed from Corinth in haste. As in
many other instances, he left running for his life. But instead of
sailing westward toward Rome and his consequent goal, Spain,
Paul charted a course in the opposite direction carrying a sizeable
collection from the churches of his Gentile mission. Having suf-
ficiently resolved the Corinthian conflict, Paul commissioned his
epistle to the Romans via Phoebe, then retraced his steps toward
Troas. There he would reconvene with a delegation of disciples from

---

1   Isa. 45:20–23; 61:6; 66:18–21; cf. Rom. 15:15–17; 1 Pet. 2:5, 9.

Galatia, Asia, Macedonia, and Greece (Acts 20:3–6). Together, this party of seven would carry their churches' financial offering for the suffering believers in Jerusalem.

Their unique fellowship served multiple purposes. Transporting a large sum—in physical coins or gold bars—would be extremely dangerous and nearly impossible for only one man. By traveling in a larger company, they could distribute monies among them while safeguarding one another on the journey. Additionally, this cooperative provided much-needed accountability. Since every region from Paul's mission was represented, they could personally vouch for the offering's transmission to their respective donor congregations.

But perhaps most important to Paul, this ethnically diverse group was a tangible witness to the Spirit's work through his gospel. By bringing Gentiles from across the Mediterranean, the apostle was authenticating his life's labor to the apprehensive, if not skeptical, believers in Jerusalem. Paul knew he needed to fend off the growing suspicions among the elders of the Judean church, not to mention his Judaizing opponents. More than merely substantial, the offering of the Gentiles would be symbolic.

When Paul arrived to meet with the elders, we can only imagine all that was said—and all that was left unsaid. James, who earlier appealed for Paul to remember the poor (Gal. 2:10), now received a considerable sum. Paul, who earlier appeared indifferent to the influential leaders in Jerusalem (Gal. 2:6), now sought to corroborate his ministry before them. Luke, who witnessed it all, disclosed only enough to reveal the tension in the room (Acts 21:18–25) but left the offering's fate to speculation. The many years of Paul's planning and his pleas for giving culminate with historical silence.[2]

---

2   There could be various reasons for this silence. See N. T. Wright, *Paul: A Biography* (San Francisco: Harper One, 2018), 350.

Perhaps that's exactly how it should be. Those who give to God often don't know the outcome of their offering. Part of sacrificing is not always seeing results. We give for the sake of Christ and his church, not for our satisfaction. And yet, when we lay down our lives like the Savior, we do so for the joy set before us. While our sacrifices for the gospel and the needs of the poor may not have a return in this life, they accrue in honor, reward, and treasures in heaven.

Giving in the Likeness of Christ

A shivering seven-year-old girl burrowed under her mother's arm. It was a snowy December morning in a small English church. The young Helen Roseveare sat in silence as the congregation prepared for communion. "*Christ died for thee,*" she remembers hearing in her heart. Her ears tuned to the rector's description of Jesus's death on the cross: "a full, perfect, and sufficient sacrifice, oblation, and satisfaction for the sins of the whole world." Later, on the way home, the alert and inquisitive Helen asked, "Mummy, what is an oblation?"[3]

Many years passed before Helen responded to the gospel of Christ's oblation, the sacrificial offering of his life for the sins of many. But when she did, she immediately sensed the call of God to similarly offer herself to him—and to the world. Not as a sacrifice for sin. Nothing, she understood, could be added to the efficacy of that offering. She could not rescue herself or others from sin by her sacrifice. "Yet there was a striving in my inner being," Roseveare recalled, "to express my heart's response to His great love for me."[4] The

---

3 Helen Roseveare, *Living Sacrifice: Willing to Be Whittled as an Arrow* (Fearn, Scotland: Christian Focus, 2007), 10.

4 Roseveare, *Living Sacrifice*, 12.

grace of his oblation once offered made an "insistent demand" upon her. In response, Helen surrendered her life to become a missionary.

Living with the demand of God's grace was also a reality for Paul. Since his encounter with the Messiah on the road to Damascus, Paul had a clear sense that God graciously set him apart—like Jeremiah, even before birth—and sent him to preach among the nations (Gal. 1:15–16; Jer. 1:5). God's mercy had come with a mandate. The mercy was free, undeserved, and unmerited. But God's grace called for reciprocation. It solicited a sacrifice in return, a price that would cost him his life.

While Paul's calling and responsibility may have been unique, his self-giving wasn't. Sacrifice isn't just for apostles or missionaries. All Christians, Paul teaches, are to offer themselves before God as a pleasing sacrifice (Rom. 12:1–2). One of the clearest signs of such sacrifice is a believer's willingness to part with earthly riches. Sharing with others is a pleasing offering and oblation to God (Heb. 13:16). And Paul expected such sacrifice from the Corinthians. Although he initially refused their patronage for his personal ministry, he still wanted them to be generous with their resources. So early in their discipleship he asked the Corinthians to give toward the needs of believers in Jerusalem—and they agreed. Later, when their commitment waned, Paul devoted two chapters of 2 Corinthians to persuade them to follow through on that prior pledge.

Paul's international offering for the church in Jerusalem was "undoubtedly one of his major activities," stretching across multiple years of his ministry's prime.[5] In line with James's request, Paul eagerly prioritized the needs of the poor Judean Christians (Gal. 2:10). In fact, he felt that the Gentile churches of his mission—

---

5   C. K. Barrett, *The Second Epistle to the Corinthians* (London: A & C Black, 1986), 217.

including the Achaian congregations—were obliged to do so since they'd come to share in the spiritual blessings of the gospel by way of their Jewish brothers and sisters (Rom. 15:27). As a result, Paul chose to leverage his apostolic authority and influence to make the offering a success. He even delayed his pioneering ambition to go to Spain—sacrificing evangelistic and church planting potential—toward the solicitation, collection, and in-person delivery of an offering designed to relieve the suffering of impoverished believers. In this, Paul's mission mirrors our Savior's love and care for us, for the needs of body and soul.

When Paul appeals to the Corinthians to similarly sacrifice for others, his impulse is patterned after the self-giving Christ. Jesus himself surrendered his rights for our sake. He willingly left his Father's side to take on flesh, to pitch the tent of God among us (Phil. 2:5–8). He became poor so that we might become rich (2 Cor. 8:9). He became sin that we might become righteous (2 Cor. 5:21). Now, in response to his marvelous grace and condescension, Christians sacrifice for others in the same manner. We love because he first loved (1 John 4:19). We give because he first gave. This is the heart of all gospel-motivated living and giving.

Challenge of Charity

Perhaps it goes without saying, but not all giving is good. It doesn't take much travel around the world to find problems with Christian charity. I recall my second trip to Haiti to teach at a small Bible institute in Croix-des-Bouquets, a large suburb of the capital, Port-au-Prince. While there, I stayed at a guesthouse that caters to short-term ministry workers such as myself. Not long after my arrival, a group of Americans showed up with a dozen duffel bags loaded with gifts for children.

After the evening meal, the group rearranged the dinner tables and began organizing their materials. When I made my way to my room, I walked past their workstation. One eight-foot table was covered in Ziploc bags full of sugary treats—Starburst, Jolly Ranchers, and Werther's—presumably any candy that wouldn't melt in the Haitian sun. The next table had its own set of plastic baggies. But these were stocked with toothbrushes, floss, and toothpaste—presumably to clean the teeth of Haitian children consuming copious amounts of American candy. As I entered my room, I couldn't help but shake my head in confusion and frustration.

To some, that group's gifts might seem innocuous, and certainly their intentions were innocent. But their good deed provides a small taste of what's come to be known as "toxic charity"—and the destructive dependence it leaves in its wake. Increasingly, Christian missionaries as well as secular humanitarians are recognizing how giving from outside sources often does more harm than good.[6] Whether it's inundating a country with donations of used clothing and thereby disrupting local textile manufacturing, or creating a market for international adoptions that give rise to disreputable orphanages engaged in child-trafficking, the state of global charity is in disarray. And when you add the explosion of missionary "amateurization"—sending untrained and inexperienced twenty-somethings to address complex issues of poverty and public medicine—the results can be disgraceful, if not deadly.[7] However, that's not to say that charity isn't fraught with problems even when professionals are involved.

---

6   See Steve Corbett and Brian Fikkert, *When Helping Hurts: How to Alleviate Poverty without Hurting the Poor . . . and Yourself* (Chicago: Moody, 2014).

7   For an example from Uganda, see Ariel Levy, "A Missionary on Trial," *The New Yorker*, https://www.newyorker.com/.

In 2011, a massive earthquake just outside Van, Turkey, leveled scores of buildings and killed hundreds of people. Almost overnight, an international, multi-agency relief effort began to take shape. By the time I arrived, many of the survivors were living in tents, afraid to return to their homes. Meanwhile, a local church building had transformed into a soup kitchen and the staging area for over a dozen volunteers from all over the world. Initially, I worked alongside a believing Turkish physician and a Canadian engineer. We traveled throughout the city checking homes and apartment blocks for their structural integrity while also providing tent-dwelling families with needed primary care and prescriptions.

Later, I was asked to coordinate teams of medical professionals traveling to the region. But sadly, as we sought to address the suffering all around us, the church developed symptoms of unhealth from within. Local leaders clashed over questions related to the collection and distribution of funds. The earthquake had exposed cracks in the believing community. Everyone was already on edge. But then the arrival of foreign investment produced disastrous aftershocks that left the structural integrity of the local church in question.

Of course, it's well beyond the scope of this book to address all the challenges to Christian charity, including the divisions it can create. Instead, I raise the issue because of the boomerang effect it can have on giving. Just as no one wants a few bucks donated on the side of the road to feed an unhealthy addiction, none of us wants millions of dollars in international benevolence to foster an equally damaging dependence, even if it's for positive provisions such as schools, or shoes, or even Skittles. Add to that our growing recognition of the historic problem of paternalism within missions—doing for others what they can and should do for themselves—and the

West's willingness to give to the needs of the global poor has the potential to fall on hard times.

It may seem counterintuitive, but in my experience, missionaries are at the greatest risk of becoming cynical, insensitive, and reticent to give. We've seen firsthand the harmfulness of charity. We also likely know some of poverty's complexity. Perhaps we've personally experienced the corrosive effect of money on relationships. As a result, we don't want to incentivize the gospel in a way that creates false followers, and we don't want to start ministries that overly rely on foreign funds. When every new believer expects help with a job, and every new congregation assumes help with a building, it creates a model that isn't reproducible. Too often the influx of outside money creates internal divisions and sets locals up for failure when the well runs dry.

Despite all these legitimate challenges, I'm also concerned for the indifference I've felt as a missionary toward the financial needs of my brothers and sisters in Christ. On occasion, I've chosen not to intervene in a situation of genuine need, then soothed my conscience with my knowledge of the dangers of a "handout." In an effort to avoid dependence, I've operated with a mindset of radical independence, keeping the sufferings of my fellow believers at arm's length.

However, if we're inclined to completely avoid the perils of introducing foreign funds into the national church, we must ultimately reckon with Paul's offering for the impoverished and suffering believers in Jerusalem. Of course, we don't know if this was more than a one-time gift. Paul wasn't necessarily creating a cycle of dependence or the expectation for ongoing support. But this financial offering was clearly one-directional. The Jerusalem church could only be expected to repay in thanks. It's also safe to assume they didn't have a detailed system for reporting the full use of monies given. The Corinthians, therefore, had to give in vulnerability and trust, without knowing the results.

What the Jerusalem collection suggests is that we cannot entirely eliminate the dangers of dependence and still fulfill the biblical command of brotherly love. Relying on others is to be expected when you're family. Taking disproportionate responsibility for the material needs of others is what life looks like in the household of God.[8] Since Paul believes that Gentiles and Jews are now members of the same family and children of the same Father, it makes perfect sense for him to call for an offering for the suffering Jerusalem church from fellow believers scattered across the Mediterranean.[9] Gentiles and Jews now have a shared kinship; they're citizens of the same nation. Paul's collection, therefore, is intended to promote the positive unity of the worldwide church.[10] They should have all things in common (cf. Acts 2:44).

If we apply this to our own day, then surely those of us Christians from wealthier nations bear the responsibility to care for the needs of our suffering family around the world. This means we will need to accept some level of disproportionate dependence.[11] Of course, we still must be careful not to give in ways that cause harm, in ways

---

8   These principles also extend beyond the household of faith (Gal. 6:10). See Timothy Keller, *Generous Justice: How God's Grace Makes Us Just* (New York: Viking, 2010), 29–32.

9   "This great collection project, so long in the planning, drew together two of his guiding passions, two strands of hope and ambition that had been central since at least the late 40s. First, 'Remember the poor'! Second, 'There is no longer Jew or Greek . . . in the Messiah, Jesus.'" See Wright, *Paul*, 340.

10   "Paul gives expression to his belief in a worldwide covenant fraternity, for which the constituent members had obligations of reciprocity." See Paul Barnett, *The Second Epistle to the Corinthians* (Grand Rapids, MI: Eerdmans, 1997), 447.

11   "Perhaps we Western Christians need to worry a bit less about creating one-sided dependency and more on creating friendships that hold hands (have strings attached). This of course, means both parties relying on the other." See E. Randolph Richards and Richard James,

that demean national believers or overlook their skills and resources, in ways that set them up for failure or are inherently distrustful. But the only way to do so is through relationships that rely on one another in a healthy (if lopsided) interdependence. In the end, we must reckon with the impetus for the Jerusalem offering where Paul "expects those of us who 'have' to share with our Christian brothers and sisters who 'have not' (2 Cor. 8:13–14)."[12] If we aren't willing to provide for the needs of our family, what does that say about us (cf. 1 Tim. 5:8)?

Sacrifice for Shared Honor

Many of us wouldn't think of giving for the sake of reputation. As such, those of us who are Western and from an individualistic culture might be blind to the persuasive and provocative ways Paul stimulates giving from his more collectivist readers. Meanwhile, those of us from gospel-centered churches might single out Paul's emphasis to give in response to Christ's lavish grace yet diminish Paul's other inducements. Our much-needed focus on Christ, along with our cultural perspective, has a way of blurring the numerous incentives Paul supplies, almost all of which relate directly or indirectly to dynamics of honor and shame.[13]

As Paul concludes his stern warning about the dangers of idolatry and immorality in 2 Corinthians 7, his tone swings again toward encouragement and hope. He hasn't given up on the Corinthians.

Misreading Scripture with Individualist Eyes: Patronage, Honor, and Shame in the Biblical World (Downers Grove, IL: IVP, 2020), 84.

12 David B. Capes, Rodney Reeves, and E. Randolph Richards, *Rediscovering Paul: An Introduction to His World, Letters and Theology* (Downers Grove, IL: IVP, 2007), 305.

13 For example, we might diminish calls for collective fairness (2 Cor. 8:13–15) in favor of individual willingness (2 Cor. 9:7). While Paul encourages a free-will offering, he also leverages social pressures on the Corinthians. See Capes, Reeves, and Richards, *Rediscovering Paul*, 165.

Their positive reception of Titus and the severe letter has comforted him. Therefore, Paul rejoices—not in the grief he caused—but in the repentance it produced (2 Cor. 7:8–9), the outcome of which demonstrated their earnestness toward the apostle (2 Cor. 7:10–12). Why is this so important? Certainly, Paul is concerned for the Corinthians' faith. But his reasoning is also surprisingly self-focused. Paul doesn't want to lose *his boast*. He desires for his labors to not be in vain. Now that the Corinthians' commitment has been reaffirmed, he has, at least for the time being, avoided shame (2 Cor. 7:13–14).

This personal—and carefully crafted—reflection then sets the stage for Paul's discussion on the Jerusalem collection. Theologically, the central reason for his offering is the sacrifice of Jesus.[14] But Paul initially nudges them to reciprocate *his own* abundant love and earnest care for them (2 Cor. 8:7, 16).[15] They should give in response to their apostle's sacrificial devotion and dependability.[16] Nevertheless, and perhaps anticipating their reticence, Paul isn't inclined to demand the Corinthians' participation (cf. 2 Cor. 9:5).[17] Instead, he invites them to join in his offering as a way to *prove*

---

14 Te-Li Lau acknowledges that the ultimate Christian motivation for ethics generally (and giving specifically) is God's grace and love. "Nonetheless, gratitude cannot be completely separated from shame, for failure to show gratitude is disgraceful and shameful." See Te-Li Lau, *Defending Shame: Its Formative Power in Paul's Letters* (Grand Rapids, MI: Baker, 2020), 166.

15 See also 2 Cor. 6:11–12; 11:11; 12:15.

16 Even Paul's logistics for the offering—whom he sends, how they collect, and who delivers it—are concerned with preserving a good reputation, acquiring honor, and avoiding blame (2 Cor. 8:16–20). Paul's ambition isn't just the glory of God or the relief of the poor. His stated aim is for "what is honorable not only in the Lord's sight but also in the sight of man" (2 Cor. 8:21).

17 Paul was careful not to overexercise his apostolic authority or lord it over his converts. However, at one time he made his expectations for the offering clear (1 Cor. 16:1–2) and was willing to do so again (2 Cor. 9:5).

the genuineness of their love (2 Cor. 8:8). His collection is a kind of test. Over and over Paul presents the Corinthians with the opportunity to corroborate his testimony about them through their generosity (2 Cor. 8:24; 9:3). By giving to Paul's collection, they will demonstrate their authenticity to churches throughout the Mediterranean. The Corinthians should want to give for the sake of *their reputation.*

Since we know the Corinthians are prone to boast for the wrong reasons, we might expect Paul to downplay giving for the sake of status. Instead, he adds fuel to their cultural fire by motivating them with the prospect of shame. Recognizing their pride in possessing and exercising many spiritual gifts, Paul reasons they should be even more eager to share in this act of grace also. Otherwise—the subtext of Paul's message implies—they could be scandalously lacking in this greatest of graces, the gift of love (cf. 1 Cor. 13).

Aside from recognizing the Corinthians' exalted spiritual status, Paul also notes their material abundance (2 Cor. 8:14).[18] The Macedonians, who were going through a "severe test" and "extreme poverty," had already proven themselves by overflowing "in a wealth of generosity" that extended "beyond their means" (2 Cor. 8:1–4). Thus, Paul's reference to the Corinthians' profusion is more than a slight tap on the shoulder of shame. Though they were rich, the affluent Achaians had yet to contribute. What made things worse, Paul had previously boasted to the poorer Macedonians about the Corinthians' commitment. In turn, they zealously responded with a kind of matching pledge (2 Cor. 9:2). Now, if the Corinthians fail to come through, Paul knows he'll be publicly humiliated for

---

18 Corinth was a Roman city known for its wealth. See Anthony C. Thiselton, *The First Epistle to the Corinthians* (Grand Rapids, MI: Eerdmans, 2000), 1–6.

his outsized confidence—not to mention the avalanche of embarrassment for the Corinthians (2 Cor. 9:4).[19]

This isn't the way we normally talk about giving, either for the work of global missions or the needs of the global church. But if the apostle's logic strikes us as strange, it would be prudent to question our assumptions about Christian charity. Giving isn't purely a private grace. Generosity can and should be a communal demonstration of Christian love and a commendable example of Christian faith (cf. Luke 21:1–4). Furthermore, while appeals to give shouldn't become manipulative, it isn't wrong to be persuasive. Nor must our motives be entirely altruistic. Yes, the greatest reason for giving is gratitude to God for the gift of his Son. But Paul can also encourage believers to gladly give for their apostle's sake, for the good of others, and even for their own righteousness, assurance, and joy.

Throughout his appeal, Paul makes the culturally influential case that participating in his offering will be to the Corinthians' benefit (2 Cor. 8:10). While we might assume he's thinking primarily in terms of *financial* benefit, his reassurances consistently revolve around the issue of honor. Of course, Paul does emphasize God's ability to make grace abound and supply (material) seed to the sower (2 Cor. 9:8–10). But when it comes to the promised harvest of righteousness—the reaping they can expect from their giving—Paul quotes a psalm about exaltation and honor for those who give to the poor (Ps. 112:9).[20] Accordingly, he culminates his appeal with the assurance of communal thanksgiving and collective

---

19 In his reasoning with the Corinthians, Paul's persuasive use of prospective shame mirrors his approach with Philemon. See Lau, *Defending Shame*, 139–47.

20 Notably, this psalm promises another blessing to those who are generous; they will have their names remembered forever (Ps. 112:5–6).

boast.[21] He envisions a scenario where the Jerusalem church receives the gift and responds by granting their *approval*. The churches of Achaia will have passed the test and proven themselves worthy. In response, the Jewish believers will pray on their behalf, giving glory to God (2 Cor. 9:11–14).

Throughout these chapters, Paul conceives of the Jerusalem offering as an opportunity for all the churches of his Gentile mission to prove their love. Simultaneously, the collection is Paul's opportunity to prove his apostolic ministry and receive the approval of James and the Judean elders. Thus, if the consequence of the Corinthians' failure to give is shared shame, Paul believes that the outcome of their liberality will be collective honor. They should give for the reward of glory.

No Less Than All

I'll never forget the first time I (almost) asked for financial support as a missionary. It was evening. I was traveling alone, having just left a conference in Chicago, and was heading home. But first I had a scheduled meeting with a retired couple whom I'd previously met only in passing. I remember pulling into their driveway at dusk and double-checking the address. As someone embarking for the first time in the overwhelming process of raising funds, I was unsettled. I had doubts. I didn't know how God would provide, much less how to ask for money. But as I entered the home of Gordy and Ruthie, their smiling welcome and humble hospitality set me at ease. Before I even had a chance to make my request, they stated

---

21 In the ancient world, clients reciprocated their patron's gift with thanksgiving. Such thanksgiving was not merely internal and emotional, but expressed itself in community by ascribing honor, boasting, and pledging loyalty. See Richards and James, *Misreading Scripture with Individualist Eyes*, 76–79.

their intentions. "We're so excited to support your ministry," they exclaimed.

To this day, I'm grateful for their quick kindness as well as their enduring support. Like so many other wonderful Christians I've met over the years as a missionary, they have a warm love for God and a heart enlarged for the world. They first give themselves to the Lord, then to us as his servants (2 Cor. 8:5). They gladly sacrifice for the sake of the gospel. Though, in the case of Ruthie, that sacrifice involves more than money.

Ruthie is the daughter and granddaughter of missionaries. Her grandparents served in China. Her parents, Bob and Winnie Hockman, in Ethiopia. However, when Winnie first became pregnant with Ruthie back in 1935, she had to evacuate to Egypt. Italy had recently invaded Ethiopia as a violent precursor to World War II. Meanwhile, Bob, an accomplished young physician, chose to remain in-country. He was needed by his Ethiopian hosts now more than ever before. The relative safety of Egypt, a sweet reunion with his wife, and the anticipated introduction to their newborn Ruthie would have to wait.

Even before the war, Bob Hockman was more than busy seeing patients and performing innumerable surgeries at the mission hospital in Addis Ababa. But with the outset of conflict, he volunteered with the Red Cross to treat the injured in a makeshift tent hospital on Ethiopia's southern front. During his time there, Bob also dug up the many dud bombshells that littered the Ethiopian countryside. Years earlier he had observed his missionary father do the same while living in China. Now, he put those same skills to work to spare villagers and soldiers alike from unintentionally detonating a still-live munition.

On Friday, December 13, 1935—just before Christmas and his previously scheduled visit to Egypt—Bob came across an unexploded shell on the roadside. Fearing another vehicle might hit it, he quickly dug up the bomb, took it to his tent, and began removing the powder, just like he had done many times before. But this time the bomb exploded. His steady, surgical hand was suddenly mauled. His side gashed. In an instant, the healer became the wounded. The physician became the fallen. The rich became poor. The young Bob Hockman laid down his life for his friends, becoming like his Savior in his death.

Helen Roseveare, after herself serving for twenty years as a medical missionary in Africa, gave expression to her thoughts about what it looks like to offer ourselves as a sacrifice. During her years in the Congo, she repeatedly had to count the cost—and pay the price—for the sake of the gospel. Later, she wrote candidly and compellingly of her experiences, the hesitations of her heart, the skulking desire for self-protection, and the difficulty of surrender. She reflected on how the once-for-all oblation of Christ still stakes a claim on all our lives. But she lamented how she, and many contemporaries, still struggled to sacrifice. As she wrote,

> Today it would appear that we Christians prefer to talk of a measure of commitment, the length to which we are willing to become involved, rather than the depths of God's immeasurable love in which we long to become immersed. There is abroad an atmosphere of careful calculation, "thus far and no further," maintaining certain reasonable limits. The carefree abandonment of love that marks the *sacrifices* of Paul, of second-century Christians, of nineteenth-century missionaries, seems sadly lacking. Today we weigh up what we can afford to give Him: in those days, they knew that they could not afford to give Him less than all.[22]

22 Roseveare, *Living Sacrifice*, 124–25.

Is Sacrifice Meant to Be Selfless?

Roseveare, like many other missionaries throughout the centuries, was inspired by the "abandonment of love" evidenced in the sacrifices of Paul. And those sacrifices were many. From shipwrecks to hunger, sleepless nights to stonings, beatings to abandonment, Paul gave more than most of us could ever imagine giving.

But perhaps among the greatest of his sacrifices was Paul's willingness to "spend and be spent" for the Corinthians' souls (2 Cor. 12:15). If you ask any minister of the gospel, they'll tell you that what Paul exemplifies is a beautiful ideal. Though it's anything but easy. To pour yourself out for others is one thing. To be constantly drained by them is another. Yet that seems to have been Paul's experience at Corinth. If you can remember back to that first sermon I ever preached, this was Paul's missionary example that gripped me as a young man. He *very gladly* sacrificed for others. He didn't just give them the gospel; he gave them his all.

Like a nurturing mother and a caring father, Paul took responsibility for his own. They were his dependents. He viewed the Corinthians as his children (2 Cor. 6:13; 12:14; cf. 1 Thess. 2:7–9). As such, they didn't need to provide for him—or be financial supporters in his missionary efforts—as much as he needed to provide for them. As their father in the faith, he took it as his personal obligation to care for their spiritual needs. That's why he was willing to return again for the third time. Paul's ministry example is one of taking responsibility and making sacrifices *as family, for family*.

But this raises an important question. When Paul made these sacrifices as a missionary, was he blissfully unaware of his needs, wants, and feelings? Was he a rugged Stoic, unconcerned with any personal desire? Were his motivations in ministry purely altruistic and his intentions unqualifiedly selfless? I don't think so. In fact, when Paul spent himself for the well-being of the Corinthians, he anticipated that they would reciprocate his love. After publicly reminding them of all he was willing to do for their sake—which also doesn't strike me as altruistic—Paul appeals to the Corinthians: "If I love you more, *am I to be loved less?*" (2 Cor. 12:15; cf. 6:11–13).[23]

Parents know this emotion. To bear the burden of responsibility. To work hard and save up. To provide and protect. To spend and be spent. To sacrifice day in and day out for your kids. To do everything out of love yet simultaneously expose your heart when you know—and perhaps fear—that such love might not be requited. Yes, you care deeply for your kids. But you realize they may receive your love—even take from you—but not love in return. This is what it means to be vulnerable.[24]

But while any good parent is willing to be vulnerable, no good parent loves without the hope of receiving a child's love in return. Such desire doesn't make our parents' love disingenuous, nor does it make their sacrifice mercenary. And the same is true in ministry. Paul the missionary doesn't sacrifice expecting nothing for himself. By constantly pursuing the good of the Corinthians, he's opened himself up to be misunderstood, misrepresented, and abused. When he refuses their money, they question his motives. When he changes plans for their sake, they doubt his sincerity. He seemingly can't win, and his love has left him exposed.

---

23 "Let the Corinthians understand that his self-support by manual labor is not motivated by a lack of love, as if to demean them. To the contrary, his sacrifice expresses the depth of his love (cf. 2:4; 8:7; 11:11)." See Barnett, *The Second Epistle to the Corinthians*, 586.

24 "To love at all is to be vulnerable." See C. S. Lewis, *The Four Loves* (New York: Harcourt, Brace, 1960), 169–70.

SACRIFICING LIKE THE SAVIOR

Yet Paul still desires their love. His ministry isn't altogether altruistic. His sacrifices aren't purely selfless. Nor does he expect—and this is important to see—for the Corinthians to sacrifice their money in total self-denial. Instead, they should want to contribute to his Jerusalem collection because they hope for a return on their investment. Paul wasn't the type of missionary who minimized either sacrifice or reward. I don't think he would stoically say, "I never made a sacrifice." Nor would he dismissively reply, "It's not about the reward."[25]

In fact, the motivation for greater reward was behind Paul's willingness to forgo the financial support of the Corinthians in the first place. As a minister of the gospel and apostle of Christ, Paul had every right to material provisions from those who benefited from his spiritual labors. This is his primary argument in 1 Corinthians 9. Yet he relinquished his rights to receive such funding because he desired an increased reward. As he explained to the Corinthians, Paul would give up many things, but not his opportunity to boast:

The Lord commanded that those who proclaim the gospel should get their living by the gospel. But I have made no use of any of these rights, nor am I writing these things to secure any such provision. *For I would rather die than have anyone deprive me of my ground for boasting.* For if I preach the gospel, that gives me no ground for boasting. For necessity is laid upon me. Woe to

---

25 David Livingstone's famous words about never making a sacrifice shouldn't be taken out of context. In the immediately preceding sentence he said, "All these [sacrifices] are nothing when compared with the glory which shall hereafter be revealed in, and for us." See Rob Mackenzie, *David Livingstone: The Truth behind the Legend* (Geanies House, Scotland: Christian Focus, 1993), 196. Furthermore, in Jesus's ethical teaching, making sacrifices in view of a reward is not mercenary, nor is it contradictory to genuine love. See John Piper, *Love Your Enemies: Jesus' Love Command in the Synoptic Gospels and the Early Christian Paraenesis* (Wheaton, IL: Crossway, 2012), 167.

me if I do not preach the gospel! For if I do this of my own will, I have a reward, but if not of my own will, I am still entrusted with a stewardship. What then is my reward? That in my preaching I may present the gospel free of charge, so as not to make full use of my right in the gospel. (1 Cor. 9:14–18)

This passage is almost scandalous. As a result, commentators often wrestle with what Paul could have meant by what he said.[26] But I find these words fairly straightforward. What might make them hard to understand is our inability to conceive of the apostle conducting his ministry in a way to maximize his reward.[27] We know that Paul was passionate for the glory of God. He was driven to sacrifice in gratitude for the grace of Christ. This led Paul to give up his rights and make numerous accommodations so that by all means he might save some (1 Cor. 9:22). His great ambition was to reach the unreached, to take the gospel to those who hadn't heard (Rom. 15:20). He was even willing to die and be damned that others might live (Rom. 9:1–3).

26 Some take the reward as internal and psychological, but that doesn't square with Paul's very public boast. Others suggest the act of offering the gospel free of charge was itself Paul's reward (9:18), but this misses its connection with Paul's reason for boasting (9:15). According to Scott Hafemann, "Paul's summary statement in 1 Cor. 9:18 is therefore best interpreted as a restatement of verse 15, with Paul's question in verse 18a taken to refer to that for which he expects to be 'paid' in the last judgment." See Scott J. Hafemann, *Suffering and the Spirit: An Exegetical Study of 2 Corinthians 2:14–3:3 within the Context of the Corinthian Correspondence* (Eugene, OR: Wipf & Stock, 2011), 143.

27 This may be a byproduct of theological emphases in Protestant theology. According to John Barclay, "the Protestant Reformers put great effort into figuring a return to God as always only a response to the one completed and all-sufficient gift, and *not* as the means toward earning a future gift or favor from God." See John M. G. Barclay, *Paul and the Gift* (Grand Rapids, MI: Eerdmans, 2015), 56. Of course, the reward Paul seeks "should not be understood in terms of earning his salvation but in the sense of [1 Corinthians] chapter 3, building on the foundation of Christ with gold, silver and precious stones." See Alan F. Johnson, *1 Corinthians* (Westmont, IL: IVP, 2004), 147.

But we must not miss this: Paul says *he would rather die* than lose his opportunity to boast on the last day.[28] His pursuit of honor and reward from God led him to sacrifice beyond the everyday apostolic responsibilities of preaching the gospel.[29] In other words, Paul poured out his life among the Corinthians for the sake of a greater boast. That same motivation led him to collaborate with his Gentile churches for the Jerusalem collection. Throughout his ministry, Paul made strategic decisions based not solely on what would reach more people but also on what would receive more praise. His desire for God's approval directed his missionary ambition.

More Than Ash Heap Lives

On April 15, 2019, a fire broke out in the famous Notre Dame Cathedral of Paris. Within an hour, flames engulfed the church's steeple, turning it into a fiery torch. The world watched in horror as the burning structure lit up the night sky in the City of Lights. Soon, Notre Dame's steeple, its iconic "arrow," came crashing to earth. But while the blaze was devastating, the building wasn't destroyed entirely. Its north and south towers, exquisite rose window, and magnificent organ were spared. However, the expansive roof, known as "the forest" for its dense wooden beams, was reduced to embers.

This is essentially what Paul envisioned of the last day. When we stand before the Lord, the works of all gospel ministers will be fully

---

28 See Hafemann, *Suffering and the Spirit*, 138.

29 Eckhard Schnabel quotes Adolf Schlatter: "The reward is promised only regarding the sacrificial service of the individual. It is with this that Paul linked the expectation of reward, without any inhibitions, 1 Corinthians 9:17, 18. Human action receives from God's action, human devotion receives God's gifts." See Eckhard J. Schnabel, "Paul the Missionary," in *Paul's Missionary Methods*, eds. Robert L. Plummer and John Mark Terry (Downers Grove, IL: IVP, 2012), 133.

revealed. They will be tested as though by flames. And Paul says that if we've built on the foundation of Christ with wood, hay, or straw, our works will be consumed. Our ministries will collect in an ash heap.[30] But for those who construct with gold, silver, and precious stones, their works will survive and secure a reward (1 Cor. 3:14).

I cannot imagine the apostle sketching such a graphic depiction of gospel ministry in cool apathy. Paul was no armchair theologian, dispassionate and far removed from the afflictions of real life. No, he was a soldier on the front lines. He had given his life in real blood, sweat, and tears to build up the Corinthian congregation. His words about the last day were intense and evocative. He was sacrificing for reward.

When we think of Paul the missionary, we might not think much about money or financial sacrifice. Similarly, when we think about his labors, we probably don't think about the Jerusalem offering. Yet Paul's collection for the poor features prominently in both his strategy and legacy. And if we consider the amount of valuable time, relational capital, and personal security that Paul surrendered for this massive project, it certainly confronts some common stereotypes of his mission.

For example, Paul can be portrayed as a single-minded pioneer—his ambition was always the next city and the next church. Yet instead of pursuing missionary expansion, Paul's offering was aimed at ministry consolidation. Paul can also be described as a dedicated evangelist who always "kept the main thing the main thing." Yet his preaching pursuits didn't override his priority for

---

30 "The tragedy is that after we are born again, we can build upon the Rock things that are going to be consumed, so that after we have stood before the Lord Jesus Christ as Judge, we have little left. This is a danger not only for businessmen but to missionaries and ministers." See Francis A. Schaeffer, *No Little People* (Downers Grove, IL: IVP, 1977), 271.

the poor. We also might envision Paul as a rugged individualist, unfazed by the opinions of others. Yet rather than disregard the "pillars" of Jerusalem, his offering shows a desire for their affirmation and approval. Paul might be thought of as a lightning rod or divisive theologian. But his trip to Jerusalem reveals a concern for consensus, unity, and a good name among the churches.

Yet these motivations can't completely account for Paul's missionary calculus. A question remains. Why would he go to Jerusalem when he knew it meant the expense—not just of money—but of his safety and freedom (Acts 21:10–13)? Why such a sacrifice? I believe the answer lies, at least in part, in Paul's desire for reward. He didn't want to lose his boast before the Lord.

In a sermon titled "Ash Heap Lives," Francis Schaeffer connects this vision of Paul and his expectation for reward with Jesus's invitation for his followers to lay up treasures in heaven. The promise of a prize, Schaeffer insists, isn't just for missionaries. It's for anyone who makes a material sacrifice for the sake of the gospel (Phil. 4:17; Matt. 10:41). And it's for anyone who supplies the needs of the poor, who provides water to the thirsty, a meal to the hungry, and a coat to the cold.[31] Furthermore, Schaeffer argues that Jesus's words aren't ethereal or purely pietistic. He offers *tangible* compensation for our sacrifices. It's as if Jesus is giving us the opportunity to deposit our money in a Swiss bank account with a guaranteed return on investment. We would be fools not to take him up on his offer.

For missions to flourish in our day, I believe we'll need to recover this promise of reward from our Savior—and this neglected motivation of the apostle. If we're to inspire a generation of comfortable

---

31 See Luke 6:38; 12:33; 14:12–14; 16:9. "Let us use the treasures God has given us in such a way that when we come to that day we will have treasures laid up in heaven and people eagerly waiting for us." Schaeffer, *No Little People*, 271.

Christians to take up their cross and follow Jesus to the hard places, if we're to stir up Westerners to gladly surrender their wealth for the sake of the gospel and the poor, and if we're to awaken a new generation of missionary heroes willing to sacrifice their all for the sake of God's fame among the nations, then I believe we need a renewed theology of sacrifice *and* reward.[32] The one who gives most in this life is the one who expects most from the next. Sacrificial missions won't survive without the assurance of reward.

I know my friend Ruthie can't wait for her own day of reward and crown of rejoicing. She's looking forward to meeting her father for the first time. She's looking forward to experiencing the sweet reunion their family never had in Egypt, knowing that reunion will now be all the sweeter and with a family even greater. She's looking forward to the prize that Jesus promises to those who sacrifice for his sake, the hope of glory that compelled her father to give his life for Ethiopia. As Bob Hockman wrote in a letter to his wife only ten days before his untimely death, "I feel sure that when the right time comes, [Jesus] will make it up a hundred-fold to both of us for these sacrifices we have been called to endure."[33]

May it be so.

---

32 See Randy Alcorn, *The Treasure Principle: Unlocking the Secret of Joyful Giving* (New York: Multnomah, 2008), 38–45.

33 Kathleen H. Friederichsen, *Bob Hockman: A Surgeon of the Cross* (Grand Rapids, MI: Zondervan, 1937), 76–77.

8

Serving Christ and
Stewarding the Gospel

Corinth

PAUL COULDN'T BELIEVE the reports. Some of the Corinthians were boasting *in him*. "I follow Paul," they claimed. "I belong to Peter" or "I follow Apollos," others maintained. But such loyal allegiance, rather than demonstrate humble discipleship, was diagnosed by the apostle as pridefully divisive. The Achaian believers had splintered into competing factions that were grasping for personal significance.

From the beginning, the mind of Corinth was bent on boasting. Theirs was a culture infatuated with status and motivated by glory. In some cases, such nobility was acquired at birth. Honor could also be achieved through individual success. Otherwise, their desired recognition could be attributed through prominent associations and social connections. But Paul would have none of it in the church. He confronted the selfish ambitions of believers who looked for identity and belonging in powerful figures.

In fact, Paul overturned their cultural pursuit of status by reasoning that he and Apollos and Cephas were merely servants (1 Cor. 3:5). They belonged to the Corinthians, not the other way around (1 Cor. 3:21–22). As workers in God's harvest, the apostles were inconsequential (1 Cor. 3:7). "This is how one should regard us," he wrote, "as servants of Christ and stewards of the mysteries of God" (1 Cor. 4:1). In the kingdom, Paul was just a household manager.

Presumably, that kind of status update didn't attract many new followers. In fact, such an admission would have been culturally unthinkable for the average itinerant preacher or aspiring philosopher. Their careers depended on projecting a more formidable image. If Paul was chasing glory—and the money that followed it—he could have done better than acknowledge his subordinate status. Better to boast in his superior education, spiritual achievements, and surpassing visions.

But as Paul continuously emphasized to his beloved church, he wasn't aiming to establish a higher rank or earn higher pay. His heart was for them. He was gladly willing to serve for their sakes. Therefore, if he dropped a few degrees in their estimation, it didn't matter. What mattered most was the assessment of his Lord. Paul served at the pleasure of the King, having been entrusted with his gospel. Therefore, he sought to please God and receive his approval as a good and faithful servant.

Paul's countercultural values no doubt upended the Corinthians' assumptions about service and status. But he also reoriented their quest for glory. Whereas the apostle rejected arrogant boasting and devalued the praises of men, he unashamedly spent his life for the day when he would stand before the Lord *and boast* (2 Cor. 1:14). He pursued praise from God (1 Cor. 4:5).

Therefore, missionaries who follow Paul's example serve the Lord and steward his gospel to receive the Master's commendation.

More Than a Missionary Pioneer

The entry in Jim Elliot's journal from October 6, 1949, reads, "Second Corinthians 1 was my morning meditation. Stirred to sober wonder at what, or rather *who*, shall be *my* glorying in the day of Jesus Christ?"[1]

The words of Paul about his boast (his *glorying*) were having their effect on the recent graduate from Wheaton College. Paul wrote that he wanted to stand before the Lord one day and have the Corinthians boast in him as he would of them (2 Cor. 1:12–14).

Taking the apostle's aspirations to heart, the young Elliot imagined what it would look like to himself appear before the Lord and have something—or someone—to boast in. The would-be missionary, who in less than seven years would spill his blood on Ecuadorian soil for the sake of the gospel, was contemplating what *his* glorying might be on that day.

There is a growing sentiment these days that questions the degree to which missionaries, or even churches, should emulate the evangelistic example of Paul.[2] Perhaps what makes his missionary model so difficult to follow, and why many today are hesitant to do so, is Paul's willingness to sacrifice his all like Jim Elliot. Yet Paul is also a tough act to follow because his method is complicated and his motivation multifaceted.

Paul was more than a missionary pioneer. He wasn't just a one-dimensional character committed to the one-directional advance

---

1   Elisabeth Elliot, ed., *The Journal of Jim Elliot* (Grand Rapids, MI: Revel, 1978), 163.

2   For a discussion of this debate, see Robert L. Plummer, "Imitation of Paul and the Church's Missionary Role in 1 Corinthians," *JETS* 44/2 (June 2001): 219–35.

of the gospel. This is especially clear in Corinth. Paul was willing to detour from his preferred path—whether in Troas, Macedonia, or Ephesus—and repeatedly delay evangelistic expansion for the sake of other, more pressing needs. After establishing the churches of Achaia, Paul took pains not just to widen the gospel's spread beyond them, but to increase his influence among them (2 Cor. 10:15–16). Before Paul could preach the gospel in Spain, he needed to *fulfill* his ministry in Corinth (Rom. 15:19–20).[3]

Why? In part because Paul views himself as a steward of the gospel and servant of Christ. He doesn't envision his mission simply in terms of what he can accomplish but to whom he will answer. Paul knows that he will one day stand before his Judge and give an account for all his labors (2 Cor. 5:10). As an ambassador, he's responsible for the appropriate and accurate delivery of the imperial good news. His obligation isn't primarily to lead initiatives and develop programs; it's to serve Christ and preserve his message.[4] As such, Paul's role doesn't require creativity, entrepreneurship, or drive so much as humility and faithfulness.[5]

While that job description may sound simple, the apostle's ministry calculus is still quite complex. Whereas he advocates for humble service and rejects arrogant boasting (1 Cor. 3:21), Paul is willing—if reluctantly so—to boast in his manner of ministry and

---

3 Paul was willing to go to Spain only after he sensed that his ministry responsibilities in the eastern Mediterranean were "fulfilled." See Paul Bowers, "Fulfilling the Gospel: The Scope of the Pauline Mission," *JETS* 30/2 (June 1987): 192.

4 Paul's fundamental understanding of himself and his missionary approach was as a servant. See Peter J. O'Brien, *Gospel and Mission in the Writings of Paul* (Grand Rapids, MI: Baker, 1995), 83–107.

5 Ajith Fernando contrasts "drivenness" with servanthood and suggests that the East has much to teach the West about suffering being integral to fruitful ministry. See Ajith Fernando, "Embracing Suffering and Service," in *Christ Our Reconciler: Gospel, Church, World*, ed. Julia E. M. Cameron (Downers Grove, IL: IVP, 2012), 208.

the results of his work (2 Cor. 1:12; Rom. 15:17). Furthermore, any hesitance to presently boast seems to dissolve in the radiant glory that he envisions for his future. Also, even though Paul believes that dependability is the benchmark of quality stewardship, it's his ministry's productivity—such as the transformed lives of the Corinthians—that contributes to his boast on the last day and currently corroborates his new covenant ministry by the Spirit (2 Cor. 3:2–3).

Nevertheless, fruitfulness doesn't trump faithfulness. Paul is reticent to trust any apparent effectiveness or rest his confidence in the approval of others. He can't even rely on his self-evaluation (1 Cor. 4:3–4). Because what appears to be a ministry success may prove to be a mission failure. Seeds sprouting and flourishing in a leafy show might eventually wither and curl. Houses built on seemingly good ground might yet wash away in a monsoon. A host of appreciable results—and even the best intentions—don't guarantee a commendable apostle. Therefore, it doesn't much matter what others observe in his ministry or even what Paul thinks of himself. Ultimately, God's approval is of utmost importance, and he'll one day commend his faithful servants. In a sense, the only boast that counts is the Lord's.

This revolutionary idea—that God will exalt the humble, honor the faithful, and rejoice over his servants—exerts a powerful influence on Paul's ministry, as it should ours. According to Paul, the judgment seat of Christ isn't merely a comprehensive audit scrutinizing every action and transaction of our ministries. We won't be held accountable just for the receipts and balance sheet of our lives. We can also expect to receive back in proportion to our wise investment. Workers in the harvest will be repaid according to their labors (1 Cor. 3:8; Matt. 16:17). This implies that some will receive a greater return, a reward that Paul primarily portrays in terms of glory and honor from God (1 Cor. 3:14; 4:5).[6] In other words, the goal for gospel ministers isn't simply to be found faultless. We should desire for our works to be proven praiseworthy (2 Cor. 10:18; cf. Rom. 13:3). As stewards of God's grace, we should invest our lives in pursuit of his commendation. We should strive to hear, "Well done, good and faithful servant" (Matt. 25:21).

Serving Others for the Right Reasons

Ajith Fernando has served for many years with Youth for Christ in Sri Lanka. Throughout his ministry, he's encountered Buddhists struck by the willingness of Christian evangelists to travel to their remote villages, visit their homes, pray for their needs, and care for the hurting. To them, Christianity is a "cheap religion." They're unaccustomed to receiving the services of a holy man without paying for it. Normally, to have a Buddhist monk come to their home, Sri Lankans must extend an invitation, provide transportation, supply a (mandatory) gift, and feed him whatever he wants. "The fact that we come without asking for anything in return and often without even being asked to come," Fernando writes, "is a powerful witness to the Christian gospel."[7]

I've heard similar observations in my travels throughout Eastern Europe. Priests in the Orthodox Church have the reputation of being in it for the money. Their positions are often lucrative, with clergy fully compensated by the state. Yet when they come to pray for a family or bless a home, parishioners are expected to provide a gift. While the priests don't necessarily ask for the money, everyone knows the system. In the Balkans, I've even been told that if you

6 See R. E. Ciampa and B. S. Rosner, *The First Letter to the Corinthians* (Grand Rapids, MI: Eerdmans, 2010), 174.

7 Ajith Fernando, *Jesus Driven Ministry* (Wheaton, IL: Crossway, 2002), 217.

want the priest to show up sober for your baptism, wedding, or funeral, you'll need to compensate him with a few hundred euros. Otherwise, you might end up with a drunk at your door. Clearly, this isn't the kind of service that Christ expects from his ministers. Shepherds aren't supposed to be hired hands who fleece the flock (John 10:11–12; cf. Ezek. 34:1–10). Instead, like the Good Shepherd, they should willingly and gladly lay down their lives for the sheep. Service shouldn't be compulsory or motivated by greed (1 Pet. 5:2; Titus 1:7).

Once, on my third visit to Romania, I was teaching the Gospel of Mark to a handful of church leaders in the city of Sighet. When we reached the critical hinge in Mark, where Peter recognizes that Jesus is Messiah, I pointed out Jesus's call for his disciples to follow his example as a servant who suffers. Specifically, we looked together at the three predictions of Christ's crucifixion. Students of the Bible will know that those repeated revelations are notorious for resulting in, somewhat comically, the disciples' bumbling confusion.

In the first instance, after Jesus suggests that he'll soon be rejected and killed, Peter pulls him aside for a rebuke. But Jesus snubs Peter and calls the crowds to follow him in taking up the cross. "For what does it profit a man to gain the whole world and forfeit his soul?" (Mark 8:36).

In the second, when Jesus again foretells his death, the disciples immediately begin debating who among them is the greatest. In response, Jesus teaches, "If anyone would be first, he must be last of all and servant of all" (Mark 9:35).

In the third, following Jesus's detailed description of what awaits in Jerusalem, James and John make a request. They want to sit at the Messiah's right and left hand in glory (Mark 10:35–37). Jesus then responds, not to challenge the possibility of such exalted status, but to question their commitment. He wants to know if they're ready to suffer like him, to drink his cup and accept his baptism (Mark 10:38–40).[8] On overhearing this discussion, the rest of the disciples become indignant. They want their fair share. Jesus then instructs them about kingdom values. They shouldn't pursue greatness like the Gentiles, exercising an outsized authority in a show of force. Rather, Jesus reminds them that "whoever would be great among you must be your servant" (Mark 10:43–44). Their demeanor and program should follow the pattern of the Son of Man who came to serve and suffer for many (Mark 10:45).

As our class discussed the series of Jesus's predictions and subsequent dialogue, we made a few observations. The disciples were clearly heading toward Jerusalem expecting a coronation, not a crucifixion. Consequently, they were anticipating honor and status as the close associates of the Messiah. They might not possess glory achieved by accomplishment or acquired at birth. But through Jesus they were hoping for attributed status.

For us, the third scene stood out as a climactic encounter, combining the twin themes of suffering and service from the previous two conversations. We also noted that, in every instance, Jesus included the inducement of reward in his call to sacrifice. Those who take up their crosses consider it *gain*. Those who become slaves seek to be *first*. In the kingdom, greatness and glory are for those who serve and suffer like the King.

Like Paul among the Corinthians, Jesus didn't reject the disciples' pursuit of status and honor; he redirected it. He didn't squelch their

---

8 "Despite the audacity of James and John, Jesus did not rebuke them directly but indicated they did not realize the implications of their request. In the kingdom the way to glory is sacrifice, service, and suffering. In the kingdom exaltation involves lowliness." See J. A. Brooks, *Mark: An Exegetical and Theological Exposition of Holy Scripture*, The New American Commentary 23 (Nashville: B&H, 1991), 168.

desire for glory; he diverted it to a later date—showing them that the path to greatness is through humble service. The way of the cross precedes the crown.

This same perspective can be found in the apostles' later writings. For example, when Peter exhorts elders to shepherd God's flock willingly and eagerly, not for shameful gain (1 Pet. 5:2), he sandwiches his instruction with the hope of glory. Peter had witnessed the sufferings of Christ and shared in his glory that's coming (1 Pet. 5:1; Mark 9:2–8).[9] Therefore, he encourages fellow elders in the church to serve, knowing that when the chief Shepherd appears, they "will receive the unfading crown of glory" (1 Pet. 5:4). They, along with all believers in the church, should humble themselves, anticipating the day when God will exalt them (5:6).[10]

Likewise, Paul instructs Timothy that servants in Christ's church shouldn't be greedy or selfish (1 Tim. 3:8). Yet he implores his protégé to embrace suffering and shame in order to avoid shame before God and receive his approval (2 Tim. 1:8; 2:15; cf. Mark 8:38). As one entrusted with the gospel, he should follow the pattern he's seen in Paul (2 Tim. 1:13–14), faithfully serving to please God, receive a crown, and share in the harvest (2 Tim. 2:3–6). In all this, Timothy should be strengthened by remembering the Christ who, after his suffering, was raised from the grave and exalted to his throne. Those who likewise endure hardship will reign with him and receive eternal glory (2 Tim. 2:10–12).

This is the consistent teaching of Jesus and the apostles. Genuine Christian service isn't authoritarian and oppressive. Gospel ministers

---

9   The glory that Peter witnessed at Jesus's radiant transfiguration included the affirming voice from the Father by which Jesus "received honor and glory" (2 Pet. 1:17).

10 See Matt. 18:4; 23:12; Luke 14:11; 18:14; Prov. 29:23.

shouldn't be like the selfish religious leaders in Jesus's day or our own, greedy and looking for glory from men. Yet the key to humble service isn't becoming an ascetic toward status for altruistic ends.[11] Jesus promises that those who faithfully serve will inherit both honor and authority in the kingdom (Luke 19:11–27). The low will be lifted; the last will be first.

Dependable Delivery: On Time, Intact, and Safe

I began writing this book about the same time as a pandemic started its spread across the globe. Outbreaks in China and Italy of a novel coronavirus, what would become known as COVID-19, soon led the United States and other countries to close their borders and shut down international travel. In the beginning, many of us thought it would only be a short-lived interruption. But within weeks, those expectations were proven unfounded. Schools were closed. Sports were canceled. The nation's economy slowed to a crawl. In the name of safety, prevention, and mitigation, the country went into lockdown.

One of the many side effects of the pandemic was a change in the way products are purchased and distributed. The public's fear of crowded spaces and an invisible virus led customers to opt for curbside pickup or home delivery. Almost overnight, businesses trying to stay afloat began offering alternatives to in-store shopping. But with increased demand in online purchases, along with the need for workers' well-being, major retailers like Amazon and Walmart had to abandon their promises for accelerated orders. Suddenly, two-day delivery became two-week delivery. A commitment to speed gave way to the more urgent need: employee safety.

---

11 Ajith Fernando notes how Jesus was motivated to servanthood by recognizing his exalted status (John 13:3; Phil. 2:7–8). See Fernando, *Jesus Driven Ministry*, 59.

When I pause in this slowed-down world and consider the task of missions—with my own travel schedule drastically reduced—I can see how the pandemic reveals what really matters. Speed is good, but it's not as important as safety. Two-day delivery is convenient, but some things are more important.

Carl Henry once famously said, "The gospel is only good news if it gets there in time." But the gospel is good news only if it gets there in time *and* intact. If it's still in one piece and hasn't been tampered with along the way. If it arrives, and the messenger isn't in danger.

This book has argued that those entrusted with the on-time and secure delivery of the gospel have the possibility for great reward. As stewards of the mysteries of Christ, they have the hope of hearing his commending word. Yet ministers of the gospel, as Paul teaches, also operate with the potential for shame, loss, and even censure. Like a postal worker during a pandemic, the nature of their work comes with inherent dangers and increased risk. They will face a stricter judgment. Therefore, in missions, speed can never be priority number one.

Over the last few years, I've had the privilege of serving with an organization responding to a different crisis in our day. It's not a pandemic. Some, however, have described it as a theological famine. And its reach, like that of Covid-19, is global. It has touched every single country that I've ever visited.

Even though the name of Jesus is spreading and churches are starting, even though movements are rapidly expanding and the mission is advancing, and even though we appear ever closer to "finishing the task," we have lost contact with our first principles. Many pastors around the world struggle to articulate the basics of the gospel and the theological foundations of our faith. They're misled and misleading others. These shepherds are ill-equipped to fend off attacks from wolves—and some of them are false teachers themselves.

And yet the problem isn't just an "out there" problem; it's an "in here" problem. It's a crisis with the very missionaries we're selecting, supporting, and sending to the nations. It's a problem with those who have been entrusted with the gospel, who should be reliable servants of Christ. As wealthy Westerners, we struggle to sacrifice financially and suffer physically. We have a long history of failing to humble ourselves as servants of the nations.[12] And yet we increasingly demonstrate a kind of false humility whereby we hesitate to boldly proclaim the gospel or teach the Bible with authority. As we've tried to start movements that are reproducible, we've not been careful to preserve the Scriptures or been faithful to teach the whole counsel of God. As we've focused on the rapid distribution of the gospel to all peoples, we've failed to secure its safe transmission. Because of this, our gospel is at risk—as are those who deliver it.

However, I believe we have the opportunity to inspire a new generation of faithful gospel emissaries who exhibit the qualities of our missionary heroes, and who follow in the footsteps of Paul. One key to doing so, I'm convinced, is through rediscovering the forgotten motivation of that great apostle. We need to inspire future missionaries to serve Christ and steward his gospel in view of God's commendation. We need to motivate them to radical sacrifice and suffering in view of the reward. We need God's approval to guide their missionary ambitions.

---

12 According to Paul Borthwick, American missionaries aren't known for their service. See Paul Borthwick, *Western Christians in Global Mission: What's the Role of the North American Church?* (Downers Grove, IL: IVP, 2012), 155.

When God's Affirmation Is Our Guide

Whenever I travel abroad, I usually try to research in advance the places I'll be visiting. Sometimes that includes studying up on local history through biographies or documentaries. To learn some of the culture, I also might peruse travel blogs or contact a missionary from the region. As someone who loves ethnic foods, I'll often look for a video series or episode that highlights some of the local cuisine. But almost invariably, I'll grab a quality guidebook that combines each category of information—language, culture, history, religion, and food—in one helpful and handy resource.

A good guidebook shows you where to visit, how to get there, and what you can expect when you arrive. It directs you to the places you know you want to see, such as the Eiffel Tower or the Taj Mahal. But the best guidebooks also lead you to sites you didn't know to look for, such as Cappadocia or Lalibela. They give the address of the Michelin-starred restaurants, but they also uncover the hidden gems. In fact, when it comes to food recommendations, I tend to trust local bloggers who know the hole-in-the-wall haunt with the to-die-for shawarma or poutine. I prefer the writers who take you into the kitchen, introduce you to the chef, explain the history of the dish, tell you how to order it off the menu, and describe the appropriate way to eat along with others.

In my opinion, any magazine or blog can impress you with amazing photos of the Great Wall or make your mouth water with glossy prints of Brazilian barbeque. But the best travel guides do more than motivate you to visit the country and taste the food. They protect you from cultural *faux pas*, language blunders, inappropriate gestures, and dining disasters. While they inspire you with glories to explore, they also shield you from danger and shame. The best guidebooks provide more than the ends; they give you the means. They supply splashy photos, yes, but they also include detailed instructions on local laws, public transit, currency exchange, and how to find the bathroom. In other words, a good guide both inspires and instructs; it motivates and regulates.

This book has sought to be just such a guide. However, I'm not necessarily trying to direct you to the best destinations or the most beautiful locations—the primary motivations for our mission. Plenty of books do that. We all know that the bucket-list items of every missionary are seeing more and more people come to know Jesus and bringing more and more glory to God. But I believe that the Bible offers us even more motivations to take the gospel to the ends of the earth. Perhaps we've missed some of those overlooked and ignored destinations on our mission. In a sense, then, I view myself as a kind of backpacking blogger. I'm just trying to point out some of the forgotten and neglected spots, the hidden gems.

When we think about our missionary ambitions—our ministry bucket list—I'm convinced we should include the pursuit of God's approval. But as we do, as we seek a mission affirmed, we'll find that by adding that destination to our itinerary, we'll potentially reroute our entire missionary agenda. Seeking God's approval has a way of wonderfully redirecting every other aspect of our missionary endeavor, because God's affirmation is more than just a glorious goal. Like a guidebook, it also directs our globe-trekking steps. God's approval both motivates and regulates our every ambition.

In the case of Paul, pursuing God's commendation was a guiding influence throughout his Corinthian ministry (1 Cor. 4:5; 2 Cor. 10:18). The hope of an eternal weight of glory enabled him to endure overwhelming hardship (2 Cor. 4:17). He was renewed in spirit despite his many anxieties and afflictions because he knew that those who share in Christ's sufferings also share in his comfort (2 Cor. 1:5). Since he believed in the resurrection—and the possibility of increased recognition—Paul boldly spoke the gospel (2 Cor. 4:13–15). Remembering that he would stand before the Lord, he overcame his fears and was compelled to persuade others (2 Cor. 5:10–11). But when those around him didn't believe the gospel or receive him, Paul didn't lose heart or tamper with God's word. He saw the invisible glory of the Spirit within, the down payment of his future inheritance (2 Cor. 4:1–2, 16–17).

However, since Paul also believed in the possibility of shame and loss on the last day, he was careful and self-controlled (1 Cor. 9:27). He sought to faithfully sow the seed for the wages promised (1 Cor. 3:8). He tried to build with the best materials for the reward pledged (1 Cor. 3:14). He even sacrificed financially to serve the Corinthians and increase his boast (1 Cor. 9:15–18). Paul also invited the Achaian believers to support his work through prayer and generous giving, knowing they would share in his reward and reap the thanksgiving of others (2 Cor. 1:11; 9:11–12). In fact, his willingness to repeatedly write, visit, rebuke, encourage, and instruct the Corinthians was so that, on the last day, they would give thanks for and boast in him, just as he would them (2 Cor. 1:14).[13]

Outside the grace of the cross and the glory of God, it's hard to imagine another impulse so powerful in Paul's life. His mission was forward facing, his motivation consistently eschatological. Paul was looking for the day when Jesus would return along with his recompense (Rev. 22:12; cf. Isa. 40:10; 62:11). He believed that,

---

13 Paul doesn't oppose boasting but "boasting for the wrong reasons." In his culture, boasting was a way to benefit others through collective honor. See E. Randolph Richards and Richard James, *Misreading Scripture with Individualist Eyes: Patronage, Honor, and Shame in the Biblical World* (Downers Grove, IL: IVP, 2020), 150–51.

on that day, the Lord will render to each person according to his works, giving commensurate glory and honor and praise (Rom. 2:6–7; 1 Pet. 1:7). In keeping with John's ministry ambitions, Paul was careful to not lose what he had worked for in Corinth. He wanted to secure a *full* reward (2 John 8).

Doing Missions When Dying Means Praise

Three weeks after writing about his *glorying*, Jim Elliot scrawled in his journal the words that would become his most famous: "He is no fool who gives what he cannot keep to gain what he cannot lose."[14]

From the reference he supplied, we know that Elliot was reflecting that day on the parable of the dishonest steward. That shrewd money manager was presented by Jesus as a positive example of those who plan ahead, who sacrifice in the present for the sake of their future, who secure friendships that will welcome them into eternal dwellings (Luke 16:9). In other words, the "gain" that Elliot envisioned was directly related to the "glorying" he described earlier that same month. He was looking forward to the day when, standing before the throne, he would join a rousing band of grateful recipients of grace and rejoice together with them in the presence of the Lord. That, he believed, was worth dying for.

One of the most well-known missionary sermons of our lifetimes, "Doing Missions When Dying Is Gain," was first delivered by John Piper at Wheaton College in 1996. In that address, he made three simple points: (1) the promise is sure, (2) the price is suffering, and (3) the prize is satisfying. Based on Matthew 24:14, Piper reasoned that our mission's outcome is secure—the gospel

14 Elliot, *The Journal*, 174.

will go to all the nations. But he then discussed the God-ordained means by which that will happen. The price of ministry success is our missionary suffering. Throughout his sermon, Piper offered inspiring accounts of believers as our examples. He referenced Christians killed in Sudan, threatened in India, arrested in Morocco, and crucified in Japan. He also poignantly retold the story of the missionary martyrs Jim Elliot, Nate Saint, Peter Fleming, Roger Youderian, and Ed McCully.

"How do you love like that?" Piper passionately inquired. "Where are you going to get this kind of courage and motivation?" You get it, he said, by looking to the prize. That's the only way you can explain someone's willingness to sacrifice to such an extent, and even joyfully accept such suffering (Heb. 10:32–34). The only way anyone can express that kind of love and courage, he claimed, is by knowing you have "a great reward beyond the grave."[15]

I thank God for John Piper and the influence of that sermon. It shaped me and a generation of missionaries. But if I could presume to add a fourth point, it would be this: the reward is praise.

What led Jim Elliot to such sacrifice? We can't say with absolute certainty. But based on his journal entries from October 1949, Elliot was contemplating doing missions when dying means *praise*. He was thinking about the eternal *gain* of having others receive him into the eternal dwellings. He was imagining what it would be to *glory* before God in joy, boasting in the fruit of his missionary life and having others boast in him. He was envisioning the day when all good and faithful servants receive God's glorious commendation. Perhaps to our surprise, so was Paul.

---

15 John Piper, "Doing Missions When Dying Is Gain," Desiring God (website), October 27, 1996, https://www.desiringgod.org/.

Yes, the apostle's mission was, in the words of John Piper, to spread a passion for God's glory for the joy of all peoples. Yet Paul also served for the surpassing joy of personally receiving glory *from* God and *along with* people from many nations. This represents no contradiction or conflict of interest in the apostle, because these two glorious ends—giving glory *to God* and receiving glory *from God*—have been intricately intertwined since the beginning. As God's crowning creation, when we accurately reflect his image and fill the earth with more of his worshipers, God receives the greater glory (Hab. 2:14). And as we ascribe honor and adoration to God before a watching world, God promises to respond by one day giving us honor and acknowledgment among the nations and all his holy angels (Luke 12:8; 1 Sam. 2:30).

Therefore, to aspire for glory from God isn't arrogant, nor is it a threat to his great name. If anything, it is yet another means toward the amplification and expansion of his majesty. As C. S. Lewis suggests, by seeking honor and affirmation from God we demonstrate his surpassing worth. Boasting in his approval is a pure satisfaction, a demonstration of our dependence, loyalty, and genuine love.[16] For a servant to pursue the reward and commendation of the Master isn't a sign of hubris; it's a mark of true humility.

This means that if we want to maximize our joy and magnify God's glory, we should live to receive honor from God. We should orient our every endeavor to the pleasure of the King. As those entrusted with his gospel, we should strive to achieve his approval and avoid unnecessary shame. As servants of Christ, we should

---

16 See C. S. Lewis, *The Weight of Glory* (New York: HarperCollins, 1980), 37–38. According to G. De Ru, "It might be possible that behind this seemingly disinterestedness [in reward] and self-denial lurks the old lying pride that will not admit man's dependence as a creature." See G. De Ru, "The Conception of Reward in the Teaching of Jesus," *Novum Testamentum* 8, nos. 2–4 (April–October 1966): 221–22, https://doi.org/10.1163/156853666X00158.

humble ourselves so that he might one day exalt us. Since we will stand before the judgment seat and give an account for all our works, we should aim to be blameless and labor for a reward. We should, with Paul, pursue God's praise.

In the end, we know the promise is sure. We can be confident God's mission will be accomplished. The question is, will ours be affirmed?

Conclusion

THIS BOOK HAS ASSUMED that Paul's ministry approach is worth emulating. I've also suggested—though without explicitly saying so—that we have much to learn from our missionary mentors of the past. The historical examples cited in each chapter are from some of my personal heroes. However, by referencing a part of their lives, I don't presume to indicate that their ministries are without fault. We must examine their cumulative work with both a grateful heart and a careful eye. Likewise, the less-than-flattering contemporary examples in some of the chapters aren't meant to fully reflect on those missionaries or their ministries. As Paul acknowledges, we can't ultimately judge before the time.

In fact, Paul himself knew his own fallibility. Given time, we might be able to identify some of his shortcomings as a missionary. But that wouldn't be a surprise to the apostle. He was aware of his capacity for error. Therefore, he didn't operate with blind self-confidence because he was miraculously called into ministry or since he was experiencing visible results. Nor should we.

Despite Paul's apparent humanity and frailty, the apostle presents himself—to the Corinthians and to us—as an example to be followed, specifically in relation to reaching our neighbors and the nations for Christ. We would do well to follow Paul's ministry method, though we should also take stock of his many motivations. Paul's ambition wasn't simply to reach as many people as possible or to preach the gospel where Christ wasn't named. One of his deepest passions, which he repeatedly refers to in the Corinthian correspondence, was his desire to receive honor and approval on the last day. Paul's pursuit for God's affirmation is his forgotten missionary ambition.

Perhaps one of the reasons we've overlooked this impulse is our cultural distance from a collectivist society driven by dynamics of honor and shame. Western missionary aspirations are largely individualistic, decided upon personally and increasingly supported by other disconnected individuals. We aren't likely to consider crossing borders with the gospel in response to the approval of local or national churches, for the sake of a collective boast, or in order to secure future recognition. We also tend to think shame is an inherently negative emotion, inferior to the motivation of gratitude or the goal of glorifying God. Yet Paul seems to suggest that those untroubled by the prospect of shame are ill-equipped to produce honor for God, much less receive honor from him.

I have tried in this book to draw our attention to Paul's pursuit of such honor as an often-ignored missionary instinct. However, there's a wrong way to understand his drive for God's approval, and therefore a wrong way to apply this book. If part of the problem I've addressed is a simplistic understanding of the apostle, portraying him as a one-dimensional character, then the solution can't be a similarly truncated reading of his ambition. We shouldn't commit the opposite error of reducing Paul's mission or ours to a project whereby we simply seek to acquire glory from God. If we make our ministries purely about achievement and affirmation, we won't be following the multifaceted brilliance of the apostle's example or reflect the priorities of Jesus's teaching.

For example, when the disciples returned from an early mission of announcing the kingdom, they were thrilled with their surprising success. As they'd preached the gospel, they'd been able to cast out evil spirits by the power of Jesus. "Even the demons are subject to us in your name!" they excitedly report. In response, Jesus acknowledges the authority and power he had given them. "Nevertheless," he cautions, "do not rejoice in this, that the spirits are subject to you, but rejoice that your names are written in heaven" (Luke 10:17–20).

Of course, Jesus isn't opposed to joy in ministry. Nor is he indifferent to his servants' successes. But his correction is meant to confront a wrong kind of boasting. There is a hidden danger for every missionary when we rejoice in what we accomplish *through God* to the exclusion of rejoicing *in God*. We should be more excited by the pleasure of knowing him than the thrill of serving in his strength. Likewise, there is a danger for those who view ministry purely in terms of what we do *for* God and, as a result, think only of what we will one day receive *from* God. According to Jesus, such an attitude reflects misplaced values. Instead of rejoicing primarily in God's power at work *through us*, we should boast in God's astonishing grace *to us*.

However, I'm of the opinion that on this issue we've fallen into the ditch on the opposite side of the road. In our desire to focus on the grace of the cross and be appropriately unpretentious in ministry, we seem to have missed Paul's motivation for joy, glory, and a crown of boasting on the last day. In my experience, our evangelical sensibilities that emphasize human powerlessness and God's unmerited favor have, in some cases, inoculated us against the hope of pleasing God and receiving a recompense for our work. Such biblical concepts now seem diametrically opposed to the Pauline gospel as we understand it. However, as I've tried to demonstrate, Paul doesn't think all boasting is antithetical to humility. Nor is the concept of an earned reward in conflict with grace.

In fact, in the very passage where Paul acknowledges his lowly status as a servant—where he states that God sovereignly produces all the growth that comes from his planting, and where he says that every field laborer is virtually *nothing*—Paul also includes his understanding that those who plant and water will receive wages according to their labor (1 Cor. 3:5–8). Those who build well receive a reward based on the quality of their work (1 Cor. 3:14). For Paul, nothing we receive or achieve in ministry can ultimately be ascribed to us (1 Cor. 4:7), yet somehow—in the inscrutable mercy and wisdom of God—we're promised honor and approval from God for what he accomplishes through us (1 Cor. 4:5).

The missionary enterprise is all of grace. Just as Paul was motivated by the grace and glory of Jesus that once met him on the Damascus road, he was also motivated by the future glory and grace that is yet to be revealed (Rom. 8:18; 2 Cor. 4:17; Eph. 2:7). On that day, God will crown those who've run well the race. And whatever acknowledgment we receive, we'll ultimately return to his praise. On that day, we'll recognize with clarity what we now see by faith, if only dimly: that all of life, all our ministry efforts, and all our missionary ambitions—even the reward and honor we receive from God—are from him, through him, and to him, to whom be glory forever.

Appendix

Questions for Churches to Ask a Missionary Candidate

THIS RESOURCE IS DESIGNED to aid churches in the process of vetting and approving a missionary candidate, whether an individual or family. The first set of questions develops categories to consider throughout the process. These questions are not deal breakers but assist elder boards or mission committees in filtering opportunities, especially when churches are inundated with partner requests. The second set of questions narrows the discussion and is meant to provide specific criteria for receiving support. A negative answer in this section would likely be a nonstarter for partnership consideration. Lastly, suggested questions are provided both for the candidate and, if appropriate, the sending agency. Churches should take a proactive approach in getting to know missionaries (and their ministries) before they're sent and whenever they return.

Of course, this level of personal knowledge and accountability requires a significant investment. Therefore, churches who take the time to affirm and send qualified missionaries should also consider a significant financial commitment to them. While this will limit the number of supported workers from a given church, it can multiply the effectiveness of their partnerships. By focusing support to fewer missionaries, churches will be able to better care for them and pray for their needs. A narrower geographic focus also allows for more consistent field visits for encouragement and collaboration. Fostering such depth in long-term ministry relationships ultimately increases the collective responsibility, fruitfulness, and joy in the work.

Categories to Consider

1. Relational Proximity

Do we know and trust the candidates personally? What is their connection to our church? Are they supported by other churches in our region or network? What is the likelihood of their ongoing relationship with us?

2. Nature of the Work

Is the work global or local? What does the work prioritize (i.e., evangelism, church planting, leadership training, Bible translation)? Is it a ministry of mercy, doing relief or development work? Is this a long-term or short-term opportunity?

3. Need for the Work

Is this work among reached or unreached peoples? Even if reached, what are their needs? Are other ministries doing this work? Do the nationals or others on the ground see this as a strategic opportunity?

4. Strategic Fit

Is this a need we are well positioned to address? Is it in an area where we already work or where we want to grow? Is the candidate, including skills and experience, well suited to this location and ministry?

5. *Collaborative Opportunity*

Would this partnership create opportunities for ongoing, meaningful ministry collaboration? Would this partnership engage our church in greater praying, giving, and going?

Criteria for Support

1. **Ministry Qualifications:** Does the candidate demonstrate exemplary character as a model for other believers? Does he or she know the Scriptures and have the ability to teach them faithfully? Does he or she have ministry training (theological and cross-cultural) and experience?
2. **Theological Agreement:** Are we in basic agreement on matters of first importance? Can the candidates affirm our statement of faith (perhaps with clarification or minor variation), and can we affirm the beliefs and values of their mission?
3. **Missional Alignment:** Do we support their ministry objectives and methodology? Do we trust them and their sending agency, or are there specific concerns regarding their understanding of the church and its mission (see below)?

General Questions for the Sending Agency and/or Missionary

1. **Church:** What is the nature and role of the local church?
2. **Commission:** How do you seek to fulfill the Great Commission?
3. **Cooperation:** With whom do you cooperate, and how?
4. **Contextualization:** What are appropriate and inappropriate levels of contextualization?

Questions for the Prospective Missionary

1. **Personal:** How is your walk with the Lord? How is your relationship with your family? With your local church? Do you have any concerns about your physical, mental, or spiritual well-being?

2. **Educational:** What is your education and training? Do you have ministry experience?

3. **Cultural:** Are you in contact with someone in-country? What will be some challenges living there? How will you learn the language and culture?

4. **Theological:** What is the gospel? What is the nature of the church? What is your understanding of other religions and the fate of those outside Christ?

5. **Missiological:** What is the mission of the church, and how does your work fit into that? What do you think of current trends in missions (i.e., OBD, DMM, CPM, or IM)?

6. **Practical:** What is your job description? How long will you stay? With whom will you work? To whom will you be accountable? How will you communicate with us?

7. **Financial:** Are you secure financially or are you in significant debt? Do you have a budget that you or your sending agency has determined? How much support do you still need?

Questions for the Returning Missionary

1. **Personal:** How are you doing spiritually? How is your family, marriage, and parenting? Where have you seen God's grace in the last few years? What made these years difficult? Are there ways we can help?

2. **Cultural:** How is your transition back? What do you miss? What have you learned about different cultures through your ministry? What have you learned about your own values?

3. **Missiological:** Are you part of a local church? What were the biggest challenges to your ministry? What discourages or concerns you? What excites you? What were you unprepared for? How have you seen God work?

4. **Practical:** Have your responsibilities or roles changed? Has your location changed? Do you plan to return? How are your team dynamics? Are you working well with others?

5. **Financial:** How are you doing financially? Do you have personal or project needs that we should be aware of? What local resources are available to you, and have you considered them?

General Index

Scripture Index

TGC | THE GOSPEL COALITION

The Gospel Coalition (TGC) supports the church in making disciples of all nations, by providing gospel-centered resources that are trusted and timely, winsome and wise.

Guided by a Council of more than 40 pastors in the Reformed tradition, TGC seeks to advance gospel-centered ministry for the next generation by producing content (including articles, podcasts, videos, courses, and books) and convening leaders (including conferences, virtual events, training, and regional chapters).

In all of this we want to help Christians around the world better grasp the gospel of Jesus Christ and apply it to all of life in the 21st century. We want to offer biblical truth in an era of great confusion. We want to offer gospel-centered hope for the searching.

Join us by visiting TGC.org so you can be equipped to love God with all your heart, soul, mind, and strength, and to love your neighbor as yourself.

TGC.org

Also Available from the Gospel Coalition

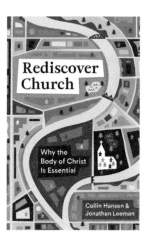
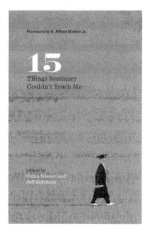
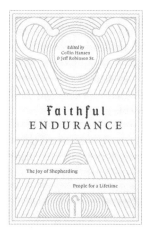

For more information, visit **crossway.org**.